COOKING
with

The Cherry Tomato Lady ™

A GRANDMOTHER'S MIX OF MEMORIES & RECIPES
JOAN THOMAS UNGERLEIDER

CHERRY TOMATO LADY PUBLICATIONS
Eatonton, Georgia

First Edition

Library of Congress Control Number: 2008943186
ISBN: 978-0-9822662-0-5

Book and cover design: Mark S. Phillips

For information regarding purchasing copies of this book in bulk, contact the publisher at the address given below.

Cherry Tomato Lady Publications
100 Camak Place
Eatonton, Georgia 31024

cherrytomatolady@plantationcable.net

www.cherrytomatolady.com

Printed in the United States by Morris Publishing
3212 East Highway 30
Kearney, NE 68847
1-800-650-7888

To My Children and Grandchildren

Some people have illuminated shelves displaying antique clocks or sparkling crystal. Others accumulate rare coins or valuable jewels to pass on to their heirs.

But me, I have little scraps of paper with grease spots on them, a bunch of index cards with chocolate smudges, and a head full of memories of family gatherings and celebrations with friends.

I've collected my thoughts and assembled my recipes for you, and I pass them on in the hope that you will treasure them too.

A Note to Readers

IN THIS BOOK, YOU'LL DISCOVER WHY I NICKNAMED MY GRANDMOTHER *the "Cherry Tomato Lady" and why I've adopted the title for myself. You also will read about six generations of our family members — from my German-born great grandmother to our nine lively grandchildren. My husband Jim and I have a large, complex blended family. Don't even try to sort us out; just enjoy the recipes and the reflections. Perhaps they will stimulate memories of your own.*

We also have a grand assortment of friends who have shared their recipes over the years. I have modified some for consistency and clarity and to offer alternative ingredients.

I'd love to hear from you after you've tried a recipe or two. This is the first edition so if you find errors, please let me know.

P.S. If you are a grandmother, visit my website and check out "Fresh from the Vine," a newsletter featuring grandchild-friendly recipes plus activities and ideas for bringing the family together in the kitchen. The website address is www.cherrytomatolady.com.

If you do not use the Internet, send me a note and I'll add you to the mailing list for the free newsletter. The address is Cherry Tomato Lady, 100 Camak Place, Eatonton, Georgia 31024.

Table of Contents

Applause

No one deserves more gratitude than my husband Jim, who has listened to my stories over and over and has eaten his way through nearly every recipe in this book (with no complaints.)

My appreciation also goes to members of the Greensboro (Georgia) Writers' Guild and the Wannabe Writers of West Virginia and Ohio. Without their encouragement, I might never have completed this project.

I'm indebted to designer Mark S. Phillips, whose patience and professionalism has been unerring, and to daughter Jenni Thomas who has lent her editing and artistic talents to help produce both book and newsletter.

And to our family and friends who have sat at our table and witnessed their love for us and for one another, I give my heartfelt thanks.

IT DOESN'T SEEM POSSIBLE THAT GRANDMA IS NO LONGER ON THIS *earth. She lived to be 98, and she had no explanation for her longevity. I am convinced it had something to do with food. Nourishing family was her life purpose. She was particular about meals and died moments after refusing food brought to her on a tray in the nursing home. It didn't meet her standards. She demanded the nurse go to the kitchen and return with a decent meal. Then my feisty grandmother left this world. It was a fitting passing: she was spunky 'til the end.*

The Cherry Tomato Lady

"IT HAS BEEN SAID THAT WHEN SOMEONE DIES, A LIBRARY BURNS *down." Reverend Edward A. Puff's remark at Grandma's funeral is etched in my mind.*

Grandma — Marie Teresa Weghorn Schillo — lived nearly a century, from January 26, 1901, to October 6, 1999. My children and I never knew life without her. Yet there is so much about her life that we will never know.

Grandma's parents, Crescentia Probst and John Weghorn, came from Germany. The Probst family immigrated first. When young John arrived in this country, he moved into the Probst home as a boarder and

GRANDMA WAS IN THE DRIVER'S SEAT MORE THAN 80 YEARS

2

later claimed the daughter as his bride. John and Crescentia had four children — three sons and Grandma. Grandma was the most durable and the most stubborn of all.

Our knowledge about her youth is minimal. Marie Weghorn idolized her father, but she had little patience with her mother. She attended school, but completed only fifth grade. She was, however, curious and spirited. Life was her teacher, and her education was extensive.

WHEN SHE WAS TWELVE YEARS OLD, SHE HUDDLED *with several families on the top floor of a school building and watched floodwaters devastate her hometown of Dayton, Ohio. At age 15, she climbed behind the wheel of an automobile and never relinquished it until she was 96. Fading photos show her posing in flapper-era outfits; she boasted that she was the first of her friends to get her long hair cut into a stylish "bob."*

One day during the last month of her life, I asked her if she had ever met anyone famous. Her eyes twinkled and she proclaimed, "President Roosevelt blew me a kiss." I asked her to explain, and she told me how she and her girlfriends positioned themselves on a rooftop when his motorcade wound through Dayton. She waved and caught his attention, and then sent him a kiss. He returned the favor.

By the time she was 19, Grandma was married and had a baby, a son Charles who would be her only child and the focus of her energies. We know little about her first husband Carl except that he was likeable but irresponsible. He disappeared periodically, abandoning his marital responsibilities. After several episodes, in spite of her Catholic upbringing, the young woman filed for divorce. Later she married Harry Raymond Schillo, a paragon of stability who saw to it that she and her son had a good life. He adopted Charles, giving him his name.

In December 1939, at age 19, Charles eloped with Dorotha Marceil Newport. I doubt Marie Schillo was happy about that. A year later, in December 1940, at age 39, however, Grandma was elated to become a grandmother. As her only grandchild, I became the center of her life. Everyone who knew her knew about me. Everywhere she went, she reported on the minutest detail of my accomplishments. I hung my head in embarrassment when I was around her friends. She even named her dog, a pedigreed boxer, for me: Lady Joan of Warwick! Thank goodness, we simply called her Lady.

Family gathered for feasts at the Indian Lake cottage

Grandma was in her glory during the 1950s after Grandpa *bought her a white frame waterfront cottage on Orchard Island at Indian Lake. Every weekend from spring until November, Grandma thrived as hostess there. Early in the morning, she produced wonderful aromas in the kitchen. Her cinnamon coffee cake aroused taste buds throughout the neighborhood. She served it with scrambled eggs and thick, fried slices of sidemeat. Some mornings she made apple pancakes, which she taught me to flip when the bubbles popped.*

At least once every summer Grandma impaled a whole pork loin on the electric spit on the charcoal grill, and while it turned, neighbors gathered with cold beers in hand to watch it brown and to listen to the hot coals sizzle as the fat dripped on them. Inside, Grandma would be baking a strawberry-rhubarb pie to top off the meal.

Homemade food was our family bond. My children Jenni and Greg, Grandma Schillo's great-grandchildren, were beneficiaries of that bond. Grandma apparently believed that without her contributions, these youngsters would be improperly fed. So during the children's school years in the 1970s and 1980s, Grandma routinely delivered quantities of her homemade specialties. She loaded steaming pots of noodle soup, hot casseroles of cabbage balls, and boxes full of freshly baked oatmeal cookies into the roomy trunk of her Pontiac LeMans. Then she drove the mile or so from her house in Patterson Park to our house in Oakwood to deposit them on our back stoop before we arrived home from work and school.

W*HEN SHE ENTERED HER 90's, GRANDMA COOKED LESS. BUT SHE developed a new passion. Grandma started growing cherry tomatoes. You might consider this a trivial endeavor. But this was a significant activity – one that preserved her ability to share with others and helped her look forward to each spring. Every March, she planted a few seeds from the prior year's harvest in small pots that she set on her kitchen windowsill. The narrow window in her tiny kitchen was magical; whatever she put there grew vigorously.*

During this cherry-tomato stage of her life, I telephoned Grandma daily to check on her welfare. And every day, I learned the welfare of her tomatoes – from the emergence of the first sprout to the transfer of the sturdy seedlings to the little plot in her back yard. At harvest time, she joyfully distributed her bountiful crop to neighbors and friends and to the women at the beauty shop.

The beauty shop was Grandma's social outlet. She looked forward to her weekly appointment with Jeanette and her lively discussions with the "old ladies" she met there. Most were her juniors by two decades, but she referred to them as the "old ladies." Between visits, she kept her hair in perfect condition.

G RANDMA EXEMPLIFIED PERFECTION. HER YARD WAS NEATER THAN any on the block. She planted eight salmon-pink geraniums in the same spots every year. Her lawn was free of dandelions and her driveway free of leaves. She also demanded perfection of others. She was one step behind anyone who entered her house: the meter man, the furnace repairman, the handyman. They could not escape her supervision. In exasperation one day, the normally stoic handyman muttered diplomatically, "Your grandmother is the most directive woman I have ever met."

She remained directive until the end, testing the patience of her caregivers at the nursing home she reluctantly entered in her 98th year. They tried unsuccessfully to win her over. One day she complained to me about several employees: "They keep coming in my room trying to butter me up, telling me how sweet I am." Their comments irked her. She looked at me earnestly and grumbled, "Now you know me well. I am NOT a sweet old lady. I may be old. But I haven't been sweet a day in my life!"

Indeed, everyone who knew Grandma was painfully aware that her fuse was short and her tongue was sharp. Sweetness and sensitivity were not among her virtues. Her sense of humor, however, prevailed. On one of his visits, Rev. Puff introduced Grandma to a young aide at the nursing center. "I baptized this young lady when she was a baby," he told Grandma with pride.

Grandma subsequently clashed with the attendant on several occasions. Later she described these tiffs to the minister and questioned, "Just which end of her did you baptize, anyway?"

G RANDMA INSISTED THAT SHE DID NOT WANT HER GREAT-grandchildren or her great-great-grandchildren visiting her in the nursing home. I suspect she did not want them to see her looking so vulnerable. But Jenni and her husband Ned ignored her admonitions and brought great-great-grandson Cameron to her room. The toddler

GREAT-GRANDCHILDREN JENNI AND GREG, GRANDMA'S FOCUS IN THE 1970S

captivated Grandma with his infectious grin and entertained her by rolling her bedside table back and forth repeatedly. Later Greg and his wife Carrie brought in Erika Marie. The winsome tot charmed the old woman. When the young family prepared to leave, Grandma – who normally refused to step out of her room – wobbled beside them down the hallway so she could show off the child who was Gerber-baby beautiful.

Grandma also perked up whenever my husband Jim visited. She was proud to have a doctor in our family. On one of her final days, with her hair freshly styled and her spirits high, she sat tall in her bed and talked with great animation. Jim politely asked about her breakfast, and she told him the same thing that she told me every morning: she had drunk two cups of hot coffee and eaten two plain Kroger donuts. He remarked tongue-in-cheek: "Well, Marie, that's probably why you are doing so well."

Every day after that, she informed her caregivers, "The doctor told me to eat as many Kroger donuts as I can to stay well."

Her favorite caregiver was a woman named Diana. Diana genuinely enjoyed Grandma's nostalgic narratives, and, in turn, shared her own family sorrows and joys. One day, Diana and I were sitting with Grandma, who was growing frailer by the day. She looked at us and said, "I wonder when He is going to take me; why has He let me be here so long?"

We responded there must be a reason, and we didn't know when she would go. Then Diana waggled her finger at Grandma and teased. "Just don't do it when I'm on duty." Grandma implied by her smile that she wouldn't. And, on October 6, she waited for Diana to sign out before she protested the food and slipped away.

We know that no one lives forever; yet our family believed that Grandma would live to be 100. We thought we would have more time to express appreciation and ask our questions.

I believe, however, that she felt she had accomplished what she set out to do; she had deftly planted her seeds in us. She realized that I would bake her cookies, simmer her soups, assume the role of "cherry tomato lady" — and pass the mantle on when it is time.

Breakfast and Brunch

INDIAN LAKE WAS A POPULAR PLAYGROUND FOR OHIOANS IN THE *1950s. On weekends, you could find your way to our family's cottage on Orchard Island by following the scent of cinnamon. This is one of Grandma's signature dishes.*

Grandma's Indian Lake Coffee Cake

1 cup milk
1 envelope active dry yeast (about 2 $\frac{1}{4}$
   teaspoons if you are using it from a jar)
$\frac{1}{2}$ cup butter or margarine, softened
$\frac{1}{4}$ cup sugar
1 teaspoon salt
1 egg, slightly beaten
About 3 $\frac{1}{2}$ cups flour
$\frac{1}{2}$ cup butter or margarine, melted
1 cup sugar
2 teaspoons cinnamon

Heat milk; then cool it to lukewarm. Add yeast. Mix and let stand until yeast is softened. Mix softened butter, sugar and salt in a large bowl. Add beaten egg. Add yeast mixture. Stir in enough flour to make soft dough. On a floured board, knead until smooth and elastic. Place in a greased bowl and cover with plastic wrap. Let dough rise until double in size, about an hour (longer if your room is not warm).

Turn dough out onto a lightly floured board. Knead lightly for 30 seconds. Punch or roll to 3/8-inch thickness and cut into rounds with a biscuit cutter or small drinking glass. You will have about 36 rounds.

Melt butter in a small pan. Combine sugar and cinnamon in a small bowl. Dip each round into melted butter and then into sugar mixture. Stand up each round side by side in a large greased angel food cake pan. (It will be a tight fit.) Cover with plastic wrap and let it rise in a warm place until doubled, an hour or so. Bake in a preheated 350-degree oven 30 to 35 minutes. Carefully and quickly, turn pan over onto large plate. Serve warm with butter. Twelve servings.

G RANDMA TUCKED APPLE SLICES INTO EVERY PANCAKE AND FRIED *them in a puddle of shortening until the edges were crisp. You can substitute cooking spray, if you wish, but do follow her instruction to turn the cakes as the bubbles pop.*

Grandma's Apple Pancakes

2 cups flour
1 teaspoon salt
2 tablespoons sugar
3 teaspoons baking powder
2 eggs, slightly beaten
3 tablespoons melted margarine
1 ½ cups milk
2 medium-sized cooking apples, such as
    Granny Smith
3 tablespoons shortening, such as Crisco

Mix flour salt, sugar and baking powder. Add eggs, margarine and milk and stir until well mixed. Don't worry about a few lumps. Let batter sit while you prepare apples.

Core and pare apples and slice into thin rounds.

Heat the shortening in a skillet or griddle. To test for readiness, dribble a few drops of water into the pan. If water sputters, shortening is hot enough. Pour approximately one-third cup of batter into pan and immediately top with apple slice and then a smaller amount of batter. Continue until pan is full. Turn each pancake when bubbles begin to pop. The second side will take a shorter time to brown. Makes about 12 medium-sized pancakes.

THE BIRDS CELEBRATED WHEN DOROTHA NEWPORT SCHILLO, MY *mother, made buttermilk waffles. She said the first waffle cleaned the iron and insisted it be tossed to the birds. I had to wait patiently for the second waffle to be lifted from the iron before I got a taste.*

Mother's Buttermilk Waffles

4 cups flour
1 teaspoon salt
1 teaspoon baking powder
1 quart buttermilk, divided
2 tablespoons melted butter or margarine
2 egg yolks, slightly beaten
1 teaspoon baking soda
2 egg whites, beaten stiff
Shortening, such as Crisco

Preheat the waffle iron. In a large bowl, mix flour, salt and baking powder. Add 3 cups buttermilk, melted butter and egg yolks. In a separate small bowl, mix remaining cup of buttermilk with soda. Fold in beaten egg whites and stir the mixture into the flour mixture. Brush melted shortening on both sides of the hot waffle iron. Ladle batter onto iron and bake until lightly browned. Makes at least six round waffles.

To me, mush is the ultimate comfort food. Mother cooked it in the evening and spooned some into a bowl for me, sprinkled it with sugar and poured milk on top. I considered it a special bedtime snack. Then she placed the remaining mixture in the refrigerator to set for frying the next morning. Be careful when you cook this; it pops up.

Mother's Mush

6 cups water, divided
1 ½ cups cornmeal
1 teaspoon salt
Shortening or cooking spray

Place 5 cups water in a large saucepan and bring to a boil. In the meantime, mix the cornmeal with one cup of water and salt in a small bowl. Add the mixture slowly to the boiling water, lower heat to medium and stir constantly. Cook three to five minutes, or until thickened. Pour into a loaf pan or a medium-sized bowl and refrigerate overnight. In the morning, turn the loaf out and cut the congealed mush into ½-inch slices. Panfry slowly in a lightly greased skillet until golden brown. Serve hot with butter and syrup. This recipe makes four or five servings, unless you eat some in a bowl the night before.

Mother never sent me to school without a "stick-to-the-ribs" breakfast, which often meant an egg dish from her extensive repertoire. This is a classic '50s recipe.

Mother's Eggs Goldenrod

5 eggs, hard-cooked
3 tablespoons margarine

⅓ cup flour
¾ to 1 cup milk
Salt, pepper to taste
Biscuits or English muffins
Paprika

Peel the eggs and chop four of them. Finely mince the fifth egg and place in a separate bowl. Melt margarine in a small saucepan and slowly add flour. Stir until smooth over medium heat. Slowly add milk, salt and pepper and stir until mixture thickens. Fold the four chopped eggs gently into the mixture. Spoon the hot mixture over warm biscuits or toasted English muffins. Garnish with the minced egg and a sprinkle of paprika. Serves two.

As a mother with a fulltime job, I couldn't devote long hours to "scratch" cooking the way my grandmother and stay-at-home mother did. I resorted to shortcuts. Bisquick became my buddy for pancakes, biscuits and waffles. Jenni and Greg were happy when they awoke to this morning treat.

Working Mom's Coffee Cake

½ cup baking mix, such as Bisquick
½ cup packed brown sugar
½ teaspoon cinnamon
3 tablespoons butter or margarine
½ cup walnuts, finely chopped
2 additional cups baking mix
⅔ cup milk
2 tablespoons sugar
1 egg
1 teaspoon vanilla

In a small bowl, combine baking mix, brown sugar and cinnamon. Cut in the butter and add the walnuts. Set aside. In another bowl, stir together the baking mix, milk, sugar, egg and vanilla. Spread half the batter in a greased 8-inch baking pan. Sprinkle half the streusel mixture on the batter. Pour remaining batter evenly over mixture and sprinkle remaining streusel over batter. Bake 18 to 22 minutes in a 375-degree preheated oven until a pick comes out clean. Six to eight servings.

ONE MORNING EARLY IN OUR MID-LIFE MARRIAGE, JIM ANNOUNCED *he would prepare Eggs Mendel for breakfast. I was skeptical as he took green onions, eggs and cottage cheese from the refrigerator. "Is this a recipe you made up?" I asked.*

"No, this is Mendel's recipe. You know — Mendel, the monk who studied peas and became the father of the science of genetics. I got the recipe years ago from a book our family had. It's Bull Cook's cookbook."

This sounded like a cock-and-bull story to me. But the breakfast dish was good, and he's prepared it many times since.

Later, I located a used copy of the book on the Internet and ordered it as a Father's Day gift for Jim. The exact title is Bull Cook and Authentic Historical Recipes and Practices.

It's a great read! Author George Herter is opinionated and outrageous. He claims the Virgin Mary ate spinach the night before she gave birth to Christ. He explains how Beef Stroganoff got its name and tells how to dress a snapping turtle (something my family knew well).

If you are not interested in cooking, he covers other enlightening topics, such as how Norwegians get rid of rats and how to survive a hydrogen bomb attack.

I've given you fair warning, but you may want to try this dish anyway. Jim has strayed from the original recipe. I prefer his version so that's what you get here.

Jim's Eggs Mendel

2 green onions, minced (or 1 tablespoon
    chopped fresh chives)
4 heaping tablespoons cottage cheese
Salt, pepper to taste
Dash garlic powder (optional)
4 eggs

In a small bowl, mix onions, cottage cheese,
salt, pepper and garlic powder. Set aside. In a
lightly greased skillet, fry four eggs until slightly
underdone; turn each. Immediately top each
egg with the cottage cheese mixture. Cover the
skillet and heat slowly until the cheese begins to
melt. Serve with toast and bacon. Two generous
servings.

DAUGHTER JENNI AND I SEARCH FOR SATISFYING LOW-FAT SNACKS. *She introduced me to this recipe that has no shortening, but tastes as if it does.*

Jenni's Pumpkin Muffins

$\frac{2}{3}$ cup non-fat powdered milk, dry
2 teaspoons pumpkin pie spice
1 teaspoon cinnamon
4 tablespoons brown sugar
4 tablespoons no-calorie sweetener, such
    as Splenda
$\frac{1}{3}$ cup plus 2 tablespoons flour
1 teaspoon baking soda
2 eggs, slightly beaten
1 teaspoon vanilla
1 cup canned pumpkin

⅓ cup raisins
½ cup carrots, grated

In a large bowl, combine powdered milk, pumpkin pie spice, cinnamon, brown sugar, sweetener, flour and soda. Add eggs and vanilla and stir well. Mix in the pumpkin, raisins and carrots. Spray muffin tins with cooking spray and spoon the batter into them (or use paper liners). Bake in a preheated 325-degree oven 20 to 25 minutes. Makes 12 medium-sized muffins.

Jim's son Matt is adept at entertaining crowds. One *Christmas morning, after the dozen family members unwrapped a truckload of gifts around the tree, he presented brunch. He served up a bubbling dish of eggs and cheese along with a casserole of baked grits, fruit, juice, sausage and bacon. The star of the meal was the apple bread. He made two loaves, one with sugar; the other, with a sugar substitute. Our challenge was to differentiate the two. Both were delicious. I've modified his recipe, using half sugar and half sweetener.*

Matt's Apple Bread

1 cup sugar
1 cup no-calorie sweetener, such as Splenda
2 eggs
¾ cup vegetable oil
1 teaspoon salt
1 teaspoon cinnamon
1 teaspoon baking soda
1 teaspoon baking powder
2 cups flour
2 cups cooking apples, such as Granny Smith,
    peeled and finely chopped
½ cup walnuts, chopped
1 teaspoon vanilla

Grease and lightly flour a loaf pan. In a large bowl, combine sugar, sweetener, eggs, oil, salt, cinnamon, baking soda and baking powder. Add flour and blend with an electric mixer. Mix in apples, walnuts and vanilla. Pour into prepared pan and bake in preheated 350-degree oven about 50 minutes, until pick placed in center comes out clean. About 12 slices.

*W*E FISH; THEREFORE WE EAT FISH — EVEN FOR BREAKFAST. ONE *summer day in Alaska, Jim, his brother Jack and I had unusual success catching salmon. We served the fish at three successive meals — grilled for dinner, in eggs for breakfast the next morning and later as salad for lunch. This is the way Captain Jack prepared our breakfast feast.*

Jack's Eggs and Salmon

8 eggs
4 tablespoons milk
1 tablespoon Worcestershire sauce
Seasoned salt, such as Lawry's, to taste
3 tablespoons butter or margarine
1 cup cooked fresh salmon, flaked
4 ounces cream cheese, cut into small squares

In a large bowl, beat eggs with milk, Worcestershire and salt. Melt butter in a skillet over medium heat. Add egg mixture and as eggs begin to set, fold in salmon and cream cheese. Heat until cheese melts. Eggs should appear moist and shiny; do not overcook. Good with fruit and toasted bagels, Serves four hungry people.

Joan's Scrambled Eggs and Cheese

We don't always have salmon on hand so I have

modified Jack's recipe by omitting the fish. To make these creamy eggs, follow the recipe above, but omit the salmon. You can use fat-free milk and reduced-fat cream cheese and these eggs will still taste good. Team them with hot biscuits and apple butter.

YEARS AGO, *DAYTON DAILY NEWS* COLLEAGUE MARILYN JARVIS *invited friends to her Oakwood home to celebrate the imminent birth of Lola Signom's baby. That "baby" has been an adult for a long time now, and I still regularly prepare the dish that Marilyn made for the brunch. She brought the hot puffed pancake straight from the oven to the table, and before it deflated, she sifted confectioner's sugar on top and drizzled it with fresh lemon juice. She cut wedges for each of us and spooned strawberries on the side.*

Marilyn's Oven Pancake

2 eggs
$\frac{1}{2}$ cup flour
$\frac{1}{2}$ cup milk
Pinch of salt
$\frac{1}{4}$ teaspoon baking powder
2 tablespoons margarine
2 tablespoons confectioner's sugar
Juice from $\frac{1}{2}$ lemon

Beat eggs by hand in a small bowl. In another small bowl, mix flour, milk, salt and baking powder. Add flour mixture to eggs. Put margarine in a 10-inch ovenproof skillet or pie pan and place in hot oven until bubbly. Immediately pour batter into pan. Bake in a preheated 425-degree oven 15 to 20 minutes until pancake is slightly brown and puffed. Remove from oven and sprinkle with confectioner's sugar and lemon juice. Cut into wedges and serve immediately. Four servings.

WHEN JIM AND I TRAVEL, MY SOUVENIR IS USUALLY A LOCAL *cookbook. By the time our trip ends, I will have read every recipe and marked those I want to try. This recipe is adapted from one in* A Slice of Paradise *from the Junior League of the Palm Beaches in Florida. Jim thought he was in paradise when I served the pancakes to him. They are smooth, flat models — similar to crepes. The key ingredient, ricotta cheese, is located in the grocer's dairy section in a plastic container.*

Jim's Favorite Ricotta Pancakes

1 cup low-fat or fat-free ricotta
4 eggs or equivalent egg substitute
$\frac{1}{2}$ cup flour
$\frac{1}{2}$ teaspoon salt
1 teaspoon vanilla
Shortening or cooking spray

Whirl cheese and eggs in a blender until smooth, or beat with an electric mixer. Add flour, salt and vanilla. Blend until well mixed. Preheat skillet with small amount of shortening or cooking spray. Pour batter by one-fourth cup measures. Cook on medium heat, turning when bubbles break the surface. Makes about 12 pancakes. Serve with butter and syrup or honey.

SON-IN-LAW NED SORMAZ FELL IN LOVE WITH MUESLI WHEN HE *sampled it the first time at the Fairmont Hotel in San Francisco. He requested the recipe, and the chef obliged by giving him a list of ingredients and measurements for a crowd-sized batch. He failed to tell Ned what to do with the ingredients so I improvised, altered a few ingredients and modified the recipe for our family's use.*

Muesli for Ned

2 cups old-fashioned oats
¼ cup chopped dates
1½ cups plain low-fat yogurt
2 tablespoons toasted slivered almonds
1 peeled, julienned Granny Smith apple
½ cup green grapes, cut in halves
½ cup red grapes, cut in halves
1 tablespoon honey
1½ cups low-fat milk
½ teaspoon vanilla

Combine all ingredients in a large bowl and refrigerate overnight. If you like a sweeter taste, top with a sprinkling of brown sugar. Serve cold or at room temperature. About eight servings.

THIS IS THE ULTIMATE PASS-ALONG RECIPE, AND I HAVE LOST TRACK *of who gave it to me first. After I shared it with Daytonian Nancy Hines, she reported that her husband Dale, a retired physician who is known more for his woodworking than his culinary skills, started making these gooey rolls for a morning men's meeting he attends. Since his first attempt at baking was such a hit with his pals, I renamed the breakfast dish in his honor.*

Incidentally, I visited the Rhodes rolls site on the Internet. I would guess that this recipe originated there, but I couldn't find it. What I did find, however, was a list of scrumptious-sounding recipes. You can Google "Rhodes Bake-N-Serv" and see for yourself.

Dale's Easy Butterscotch Rolls

Cooking spray
¾ cup chopped walnuts or pecans
18 frozen white dinner rolls, such as Rhodes

1 package (3½ ounces) cook-and-serve
    butterscotch pudding mix (not instant)
½ cup butter or margarine
½ cup dark brown sugar
1 teaspoon cinnamon

Lightly coat a Bundt pan with cooking spray. Sprinkle nuts in bottom of the pan. Pile frozen rolls on top of nuts. Sprinkle pudding mix over rolls. In a small pan, heat butter, brown sugar and cinnamon until melted. Pour warm mixture over rolls. Keep uncovered on kitchen counter overnight. The next morning bake in a preheated 350-degree oven for 25 to 30 minutes. Turn onto serving plate. Serves eight generously.

FORMER DAYTONIANS TOM AND KAY BECKETT ARE ADVENTUROUS *friends. In their professional lives, Kay was a certified public accountant, and Tom was a hospital administrator. Jim and I met him when he was president of St. Elizabeth Medical Center in Dayton.*

After retiring, the couple fulfilled their life dream by taking up residence for three years aboard their sailboat "Suncatcher." As liveaboards, they simplified their lifestyle and shared all responsibilities – good lessons for the rest of us.

Now they reside on terra firma in Hendersonville, North Carolina, but continue sharing household tasks such as cooking. Tom made this dish for brunch when we visited. He attributes the recipe to friends Jack and Rita Eaton.

Tom's Tomato Pie

2 cups baking mix, such as Bisquick
¼ pound butter, softened
6 tablespoons hot water

3 medium tomatoes, sliced
Dried oregano
Dried basil
Onion powder
Cayenne pepper
Salt, pepper
1 cup mayonnaise
1 cup sharp cheddar, shredded
Dill weed

Combine baking mix, butter and water in a medium-sized bowl. Adjust the water and baking mix as needed to make appropriate consistency for rolling. Form into a ball and roll into a circle large enough to fill a 9-inch pie plate. Line pie plate with pastry, prick with a fork and bake 15 minutes.

After baking, line the pastry shell with sliced tomatoes and sprinkle with seasonings (except dill) to taste. Mix mayonnaise and cheddar in a small bowl and spread on top of the tomatoes. Sprinkle with dill weed. Bake in a preheated 350-degree oven for about 45 minutes. Six servings.

Don't think for a moment that the Becketts' adventures *ebbed when they moved onto land. They switched from sailing East Coast waterways to cruising the countryside on their flashy "hawg."*

Their plush motorcycle is equipped with roomy baggage compartment and a dashboard that resembles an airplane control panel. Here's to active retirement living and Kay's breakfast favorite.

Kay's Bacon and Eggs Pancake

3 strips bacon, fried crisp and chopped (reserve
    the grease)

3 eggs, beaten
2 cups milk
1 cup sifted flour
2 tablespoons sugar
1 ½ teaspoons salt

Fry bacon in a 9 or 10-inch ovenproof skillet. Lift strips out, retaining the grease in the pan. Chop the bacon and return to skillet. In a bowl, combine eggs and milk. Add sifted flour, sugar and salt and beat by hand or on low setting of electric beater until smooth (do not overbeat). Pour mixture over bacon and grease in the skillet. In a preheated 375-degree oven, bake 40 minutes or until inserted knife comes out clean. Serve in wedges with butter and syrup. Six servings.

*M*Y INTRODUCTION TO STRATA TOOK PLACE AT THE HOME OF *fellow journalist Peggy Magill. She hosted a farewell brunch when I left suburban journalism at the* Kettering-Oakwood Times *for an editor's post at the* Dayton Daily News. *Her version was prepared with ham. This is a lighter, but reasonably rich, variation.*

Strata ala Peggy

3 eggs
2 cups milk
¼ teaspoon dry mustard
1 teaspoon Worcestershire sauce
1 teaspoon salt
½ teaspoon pepper
1 ½ pounds ground turkey sausage, browned
    and crumbled
6 slices bread
2 cups cheddar cheese, shredded

In a bowl, combine eggs, milk, mustard, Worcestershire, salt and pepper. Place half the browned and cooled sausage in a 13x9x2-inch baking pan. Cover with bread slices. Top bread with remaining sausage and the shredded cheese. Pour egg mixture over all. Cover with foil and refrigerate overnight. Bake covered at 350 degrees for 30 minutes or until a knife inserted in the center comes out clean. Eight to 10 servings.

STATISTICS SHOW THAT SECOND MARRIAGES ARE RISKY ENDEAVORS. *So before we exchanged vows, Jim and I had heart-to-heart discussions about family relationships, managing money and the division of household labor. We also discussed food. Jim made me solemnly promise to never serve "SOS" at our table. I've upheld the oath, but just in case you want to try this popular dish from the 1950s, here it is. If you don't know what "SOS" means, don't ask.*

SOS for Anyone but Jim

2 tablespoons butter or margarine
2 tablespoons minced onion
2 tablespoons flour
1 cup milk (low-fat is fine)
4 ounces dried beef, torn into small pieces (or
    4 ounces browned ground beef)
Pepper to taste
Dash garlic powder (optional)

Melt butter in a skillet and add onion. Cook over medium heat until onions are soft. Slowly add flour to the mixture and then slowly stir in the milk. Simmer, stirring, until sauce thickens. Add dried beef, pepper and garlic powder. Spoon over toast or English muffins. Serves two.

O HIOANS FOR MOST OF OUR LIVES, JIM AND I CHOSE CLIMATE-*friendly Georgia for retirement living. One day we were dirt-covered and sweaty from pruning and weeding when new Georgia friends, Maura and Frank Lanzarone pulled into our driveway.*

"We brought you some bagels," said Maura, handing me a brown paper bag, warm on the bottom. She made the bagels herself. I never before met anyone who made bagels, and I never met anyone like Maura, who moved to the South from Connecticut. At an age when others were retiring, she signed up for a prestigious culinary school in New York City, fulfilling her desire to become a chef. Her bagels have an appealing chewy texture.

Some Sunday morning, try making bagels instead of buying them at the deli. I think you'll be glad you did.

Maura's Bagels

Dough
2 teaspoons cornmeal
2 envelopes dry yeast or $1\frac{1}{2}$ ounces compressed
    yeast
$1\frac{1}{2}$ cups warm water
5 cups bread flour
4 tablespoons sugar
2 teaspoons salt

Water bath
2 quarts water
4 teaspoons sugar

Topping
Sesame seeds, poppy seeds or coarse salt

Preheat the oven to 400 degrees. Prepare two sheet pans by lining them with parchment paper and sprinkling cornmeal on top to prevent the bagels from sticking.

Dissolve yeast in water and let stand 10 minutes. Reserve about ½ cup of the flour. Then combine remaining flour with the salt and sugar in a large bowl. Make a well in the center. Add the yeast liquid and knead until a dough forms. The dough should be firm and not sticky. Add reserved flour a small bit at a time as necessary. Turn the dough onto a lightly floured surface, kneading until the dough is smooth. Sprinkle additional reserved flour on the board as needed to prevent sticking. Cover the dough with a clean tea towel, allowing it to rest while you prepare the boiling water bath.

Bring the water to a boil and add the sugar to it. Meanwhile, divide the dough into 12 equal pieces. Roll each piece into a rope about 10 inches long. Moisten the ends and wrap them together, making a bagel shape. Place them on the prepared pans and cover them with a tea towel. "Proof" (that means let them rise) the bagels for 10 minutes; do not let them rise much longer than this.

Place bagels, a few at a time, in simmering water for about 30 seconds. Remove and place back on the parchment. Immediately sprinkle with choice of toppings.

Bake immediately for 15 minutes in a preheated 400-degree oven, until golden and set. Cool on rack. Makes 12 bagels.

A FEW YEARS AGO, JIM CONVINCED OUR CLOSE FRIENDS FROM *Dayton — Mike and Susan Craig and Dale and Nancy Hines — that a biking vacation would be a hoot. He had some trouble convincing me of that, but I finally agreed. We were all in our sixties.*

I had not pedaled much since my teenage years. But I trained (as did our friends) and managed to work my way up to riding 19 miles a day on flat Georgia roads near our home. By comparison, exercise enthusiast Jim, at age 65, had been on a biking kick for several years and could travel 50 miles at a time without hurting too much.

This eager group flew off to Bar Harbor, Maine, on an excursion that was billed for bikers at beginner to intermediate levels. Well, you can't convince me that those routes with bumpy brick roads, steep inclines and speeding semi's were for beginners. I huffed and puffed through the five days with more time logged in the sag wagon than anyone else—but I did have fun.

Best of all, after the exercise we could eat whatever we wanted with no remorse. One chilly day, with raindrops dripping down our helmets and goose bumps rising on our extremities, we filed into the dining room of the Jordan Pond House and devoured steaming bowls of chowder and platters of hot popovers.

Now Jim and I make popovers for breakfast guests. If you want to make them, buy a popover pan at a kitchen supply shop. You can use a cupcake tin, but the results won't be so spectacular. This recipe makes enough batter for a popover pan with six cups. Be sure to serve the popovers immediately after baking, and top them with real butter and jam or honey.

Biker Popovers

1 ¼ cups flour
¼ teaspoon salt
3 large eggs
1 tablespoon butter, melted
1 ¼ cups milk (use 2 percent or whole milk
    for best results)
Cooking spray
2 tablespoons butter, cut into 6 pieces

Place oven rack in the middle of the oven and preheat oven to 400 degrees. In a blender, combine flour, salt, eggs, melted butter and milk and blend until smooth.

(If you use an electric mixer, beat about two minutes.) Spray the popover pan with cooking spray and place in the heated oven for about a minute and a half. Remove the pan from the oven and place one piece of butter into each cup and put the pan back into the oven for about one minute until the butter bubbles. Fill each cup one-half to two-thirds full with batter and bake 20 minutes. Reduce temperature to 300 degrees (don't open the oven door!) and continue baking 20 minutes. Makes six popovers. You can make the batter ahead of time and keep it in the refrigerator, but bring it to room temperature before you bake it.

JOAN MILES, WHO RELOCATED WITH HUSBAND DAVID FROM *Michigan to Reynolds Plantation in Georgia, maintains a picture-perfect home and prepares meals just as meticulously. She likes to add personal touches to recipes she finds on the Internet as she did with this sweet bread. One Christmas holiday, she made numerous loaves and presented them to appreciative friends. If you don't have pumpkin pie spice on hand, Joan suggests mixing two tablespoons each of cloves, cinnamon, allspice and one teaspoon of ground ginger. That will be enough spice for a number of loaves.*

Joan M's Pumpkin-Cranberry Loaves

3 cups flour
1 tablespoon plus 2 teaspoons pumpkin
    pie spice
2 teaspoons baking soda
1 ½ teaspoons salt
1 ½ cups sugar
1 ½ cups no-calorie sweetener, such as Splenda
1 can (15 ounces) pumpkin
4 large eggs
½ cup vegetable oil

$\frac{1}{2}$ cup applesauce
$\frac{1}{2}$ cup orange juice or water
1 cup sweetened, dried cranberries
$\frac{3}{4}$ cup pecans or almonds, chopped

Combine flour, pumpkin pie spice, baking soda and salt in large bowl. Combine sugar, sweetener, pumpkin, eggs, oil, applesauce and juice in large bowl and beat with electric mixer until just blended. Add pumpkin mixture to flour mixture and stir until just moistened. Fold in cranberries and nuts. Spoon into two greased loaf pans.

Bake in preheated 350-degree oven for 60 to 65 minutes, or until pick inserted in middle comes out clean. Cool in pans on wire rack for 10 minutes; then remove from pans and allow to fully cool on racks. Yields two loaves.

DAUGHTER JENNI AND SON GREG'S FATHER, JOHN THOMAS, WAS *reared in New Concord, Ohio, where his parents Scott and Frances Thomas grew vegetables and a bountiful crop of big juicy strawberries in their garden. "Mom" transformed the strawberries into sweet shimmering freezer jam; I suspect her recipe was from a pectin box. When we visited, she always dug into the depths of her freezer and brought out a container for us to take home. This jam is perfect on popovers.*

Frances' Freezer Jam

7 one-cup glass jars or rigid plastic containers
    with tight lids
5 cups fresh strawberries
7 cups sugar (no substitutions)
$\frac{3}{4}$ cup water

1 envelope fruit pectin, such as Sure-Jell

Wash and scald the containers and lids. Wash the berries, remove the green caps and mash them in a large bowl. Add sugar and stir well. Let stand 10 minutes. Mix water and pectin in a small pan. Bring to a full boil and boil one minute, constantly stirring. Immediately add to the fruit and stir constantly for three minutes. Immediately ladle into containers, leaving about one-half inch of space on top. With a paper towel, wipe the edges of the containers. Cover immediately with lids. Let stand at room temperature 24 hours. Place in freezer. Unfrozen jam can be kept in the refrigerator about three weeks. Makes seven cups.

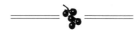

Legacy

IT HAS TAKEN ME A LIFETIME TO COME TO TERMS WITH MY FATHER. *He wasn't perfect, not even close. He drank too much, too often. He couldn't manage money, he was too restless to keep a job and he had a temper that I feared.*

But he was a convivial host and an ardent chef who wanted to make sure that his only child wouldn't turn into a meatloaf-and-potatoes plebian. With exuberance, he introduced Mother and me to new foods.

One evening in the early 1950s, he rushed into the house carrying a big, flat, hot-to-the-touch square box. He called to Mother to set out plates and silverware, and she and I hurried into the kitchen as he placed the cardboard container on the wooden table in our dining alcove. A spicy essence invaded the room when he pushed the lid back to reveal a giant disk of bread layered with red sauce, melted cheese and thin rounds of some type of meat. We didn't know what it was.

"It's the newest thing," he announced. "Pizza pie." He had purchased it in a shop where some folks named Cassano assembled these oversized pies and baked them in huge ovens. He convinced us that Italians ate them for dinner. We took a tentative taste and then savored every slice of pepperoni and every crumb from the crust.

BESIDES HIS INTEREST IN FOOD, MY FATHER WAS INFATUATED WITH *electric kitchen gadgets. We were the first family in the 1700 block of Grand Avenue to own an electric blender, an electric knife sharpener and an electric egg poacher, which cooked three eggs at a time, one for each of us.*

He ceremoniously brought home other modern contrivances. He bought Mother an ironer, a hooded mechanism that took up a lot of space in her cramped kitchen. In those days, Mother ironed our sheets and pillowcases and even Daddy's boxer shorts. The "mangle," as this machine was called, made quick work of these chores. On Mother's Day, he presented her with an electric manicure set — at a time when we still were using the gas flame on our kitchen stove to heat our hair curling iron. We got an electric curling iron later.

In contrast to his absorption with contemporary foods and gadgets, Daddy steeped himself in ethnic cookbooks and practiced "old-country" cooking. He made "head cheese." (You don't want to know much about this, but, yes, an animal's head was involved.) He shredded vast amounts of cabbage, which he stored in deep earthenware crocks in our cool basement until it fermented and turned into sauerkraut. In his garden plot, he grew ugly gnarled roots, dug them up, grated them and added a splash of gin to produce horseradish so potent that one sniff made you teary-eyed.

MY FATHER PRESIDED OVER HOLIDAY MEALS. THANKSGIVING WAS *the most elaborate — from picturesque appetizers and relish platters to the belt-busting desserts. With Hollywood flair, Daddy presented jumbo shrimp cocktails in his finest tall-stemmed martini glasses and circulated plates of ripe olives, radish roses and cubes of sharp cheese and kosher salami mounted on frilly toothpicks. Next, he brought out tossed salad with homemade chunky blue cheese dressing, hot yeast rolls and creamery butter. Then he spooned caramelized sweet potatoes and mounds of butter-streaked mashed potatoes onto our plates along with thick slabs of white meat and thinner slices of dark meat from the massive tom he had tended since dawn. In the meantime, we passed a heaping bowl of moist stuffing and a boatful of giblet gravy. The meal was rounded out with green bean casserole and succotash made by Mother and me and with scalloped oysters contributed by Grandma. Cranberry sauce was the only food that came from a can. Mother preferred the smooth version you jiggled out of the tin and sliced into neat circles.*

After downing seconds of almost everything, we paused while Mother made tea. Sometimes, we played Monopoly to "let our stomachs rest." But soon Daddy displayed the desserts — walnut-stuffed dates coated with powdered sugar, a hot double-crusted mincemeat pie, and a nutmeg-garnished pumpkin pie piled high with freshly whipped sweet cream. Then he would break open a package of Esther Price chocolates produced at the Dayton candy emporium, and we would select our favorites. Mine were caramels dipped in milk chocolate.

That was our feast: a lavish spread prepared every November for five people. That's right — five people. While other families had

<small>DADDY AND MOTHER RELAXING AFTER A THANKSGIVING MEAL AT THE COTTAGE</small>

elbow-rubbing crowds on holidays, five of us gathered at our table – Mother, Daddy, Grandpa, Grandma and me.

Daddy spent more time in our kitchen than in any other room of the house. For him, the kitchen was a refuge, a spot where he had his most thoughtful hours. He would study at the kitchen table in our cozy alcove. As I advanced in school, he sometimes asked me to help him pronounce a word. He had only an eighth-grade education, but he was hungry for knowledge. He never had a class in a foreign language, but he once read "The Three Musketeers" in French with my assistance and aid from his trusty English-French dictionary.

Daddy never knew his blood father, and I believe this troubled him until his dying day. Discontent most of his life, he was always searching, trying to reach some peace within. Although baptized a Catholic, he labeled himself agnostic and was cynical about religion;

yet he read stacks of books on religion and philosophy.

One Sunday afternoon, he invited me to join him in the alcove. For days, he had been poring over books on the power of the mind. Not knowing what to expect, I sat beside him on the wooden bench as he folded a small square of white paper and balanced it on the head of a needle that he had stuck in a cork.

"Now watch this carefully, Joan," he said, slowly folding his hands in his lap. "I am going to move this paper to the right with my mind." I watched him focus, and I saw the paper turn! Then he said, "Now I am going to turn the paper to the left." I witnessed the paper reverse its direction. I didn't tell anyone what I had seen, not even my mother, but I will never forget it.

Many years have passed since we shared a meal or talked in the shelter of our kitchen. Time has helped to heal the bruises that his harsh words and careless actions left on my heart. Now I am grateful for the appreciation of good food that he passed on to me; but most of all, I am thankful for the power he unleashed the day his mind turned that scrap of paper.

Appetizers and Beverages

T HE SCHILLO FAMILY NEVER CONSIDERED BUYING BOTTLED COCKTAIL sauce. *Daddy concocted his own, varying the ingredients according to what was on hand. Sometimes he used chili sauce instead of catsup; sometimes he added cayenne pepper. This was his most common mixture.*

Daddy's Shrimp Cocktail Sauce

    1 cup catsup
    1 tablespoon horseradish
    1 teaspoon fresh lemon juice
    Dash of Tabasco sauce

Mix all ingredients and chill at least two hours. To serve, line large martini glasses with leaf lettuce. Place several large cooked, peeled shrimp with tail up in each glass. Spoon a generous dollop of sauce on top. Add a wedge of lemon on the side. Place glasses on saucers with a couple of saltines.

D ADDY MADE EVEN LUNCH MEAT AND CHEESE APPEALING BY *threading them on toothpicks with cellophane ruffles. Wine shops and specialty markets generally have a selection of fancy picks. Here are some combinations to try.*

Daddy's Toothpick Tidbits

    Chunk of salami, chunk of Swiss cheese, baby
        gherkin (sweet midget pickle)
    Cherry tomato, chunk of havarti, pitted ripe olive
    Piece of cocktail weiner, slice of dill pickle,
        wedge of cheddar
    Chunk of Gouda, square of ham, stuffed olive

CHOPPED CHICKEN LIVERS RANKED HIGH ON DADDY'S LIST OF HORS d'oeuvres. *In the 1950s the dish was a fashionable food. It has fallen from grace in recent years because of the cholesterol content, but I succumb to temptation about once a year.*

Daddy's Chopped Chicken Livers

$\frac{1}{2}$ pound chicken livers, rinsed and trimmed
1 teaspoon onion, finely chopped
2 tablespoons mayonnaise
$\frac{1}{4}$ teaspoon salt
Dash of pepper
Dash of garlic powder (optional)

Broil livers for about 15 minutes, turning once. Cool and chop. Add onion, mayonnaise and seasonings. Chill. To serve, line individual cocktail plates with leaves of lettuce and top each with a mound of the livers. Add a couple of saltines to the plate. Four appetizer servings.

A SECOND CHICKEN LIVER DISH THAT DADDY PREPARED WAS *rumaki. My guess is that he tasted it at the Tropics, a popular Dayton restaurant in the 1950s, and then duplicated the recipe at home. If you don't like chicken livers, omit them. Bacon-wrapped water chestnuts are good appetizers. These are broiled, but you can grill them or prepare them in the microwave.*

Daddy's Rumaki

About $\frac{3}{4}$ pound chicken livers
1 can (8 ounces) whole water chestnuts
$\frac{1}{2}$ cup soy sauce

1 tablespoon honey
Dash of garlic powder
12 slices of bacon, cut in half crosswise
Wooden toothpicks

Rinse the livers in cold water, drain them and cut them into bite-sized pieces. Drain the water chestnuts. In a small, deep bowl, combine soy sauce, honey and garlic powder.

Take a piece of liver and a water chestnut and wrap the two with a piece of bacon. Secure with a toothpick. Repeat until you have used all the livers. Place them in a bowl or baking pan and spoon the marinade over them. Cover and chill at least two hours, turning them now and then.

Broil about four inches from the heat for 6 to 8 minutes, turning once. They will be done when the bacon is crisp and the liver is no longer pink. Serve immediately. Makes about 24 appetizers.

N O ONE KEEPS CLOSER TABS ON THE UNGERLEIDER FAMILY THAN *Cheri Ungerleider Crothers, Jim's cousin. A devoted genealogist, she has delved into complex family links. She also has preserved some family recipes. She helped fine-tune this one with her mother (Jim's Aunt Gertrude), Aunt Elva (married to Clyde Graham Sr.), and Cheri's Aunt Florence (Jim's mother).*

Ungerleiders' Chicken Liver Pate

Olive oil to cover skillet (or use chicken fat)
1 medium yellow onion, chopped
1 pound chicken livers, rinsed and trimmed
About 1 tablespoon brandy

4 hard-boiled eggs, chopped
4 tablespoons Hellman's mayonnaise (no other
    brand will do, according to this family)
Salt, pepper

Fry onions in the oil until golden. Remove the pan
from the stove and add livers and brandy. Saute
livers until they are thoroughly cooked (no pink
when cut). Place mixture in food processor. Add
eggs and blend slightly, leaving some small chunks.
Remove to bowl. Add mayonnaise and salt and
pepper to taste. Chill at least three hours. Check
seasoning before serving. Serve with assorted
crackers. Eight to 10 servings.

IN MY WEIGHT-CONSCIOUS GENERATION, FRIENDS FAVORED
*appetizers that were lighter than those served by my parents. This
is an old standby of mine that can be assembled early in the day.*

Stuffed Button Mushrooms

½ pound fresh button mushrooms of uniform
    size
1 celery rib, finely chopped
1 tablespoon onion, finely chopped
1 teaspoon Worcestershire sauce
¼ teaspoon garlic powder
¼ teaspoon seasoned salt, such as Lawry's
4 ounces margarine
¼ cup cracker crumbs

Clean mushrooms and remove stems. Chop stems and
place in a bowl with celery, onions, Worcestershire,
garlic powder and salt. Mix. Melt margarine in a
skillet and add vegetable mixture. Heat on medium

until onion and celery are soft. Add cracker crumbs. Place mushroom caps on a lightly greased baking sheet and fill each with vegetable-crumb mixture. Bake at 350 degrees about 10 minutes, until mushrooms have softened and mixture is hot. Makes about 15 appetizers, depending on size of mushrooms.

D RIED BEEF IS RELATIVELY LOW IN FAT. A SERVING OF SEVEN SLICES *has 1.5 grams of fat and 60 calories. It's high in sodium, however, so rinse the slices and drain them before you use the meat. You can substitute thin slices of turkey or ham if you prefer. It's impossible to eat dried beef without thinking of my elementary and high school pal and college roomie – Judi Niehaus Fenson. She packed a dried beef sandwich for lunch almost every day when we went to Colonel White High School. My sandwich was peanut butter or bologna. She's still thinner than I.*

Dried Beef and Cheese Rollups

1 package (3 ounces) low-fat cream cheese at
    room temperataure
½ teaspoon Worcestershire sauce
Dash of garlic powder
1 package or jar (about 2 ounces) dried beef
    slices
Baby gherkins (midget pickles), optional

Combine cream cheese, Worcestershire sauce and garlic powder. Spread a spoonful of the mixture on a slice of dried beef. Bring opposite sides to the center and roll up. Secure with a fancy toothpick and add a midget pickle on top if you like. Chill before serving. Makes 12 to 14 small appetizers.

Y OU WILL BE REWARDED WITH AN ABUNDANCE OF FRUIT WHEN YOU *begin planting cherry tomatoes. Tomatoes, botanically, are fruit; however, in 1893, the United States Supreme Court, for tax reasons, ruled them a vegetable. (No wonder we're confused.) Five of them add up to only 20 calories and they are a good source of Vitamin C.*

Stuffed Cherry Tomatoes

Wash tomatoes, remove tops and scoop out the seeds. Spoon in any of the fillings below or make up your own.

Pimiento cheese
Cream cheese, softened, with a dash of oregano
    and garlic powder added
Guacamole
Pesto
Goat cheese, softened, with a bit of crushed
    rosemary and thyme added
Blue cheese topped with half a walnut
Hummus

H ERE'S ANOTHER GOOD WAY TO USE YOUR CROP OF CHERRY *tomatoes. This is a light, fresh-tasting appetizer to serve before a meal of pasta. Leftover mixture makes a good topping for a tossed salad.*

Minty Tomato Spread

1 pound diced cherry tomatoes (if you use large
    tomatoes, seed them before dicing)
1 roasted red bell pepper, finely diced (canned
    is fine)
2 ounces feta cheese, crumbled
$\frac{1}{4}$ cup thinly sliced fresh basil

¼ cup minced sweet onion, such as Vidalia
¼ cup finely chopped fresh mint
1 teaspoon olive oil
Salt, pepper to taste
Toasted French bread slices, pita bread or
    Belgian endive leaves

Combine all ingredients. Refrigerate several hours. Spread onto toasted slices of bread, or for a more unusual presentation, spoon into Belgian endive leaves.

K AREN AND WAYNE BAIN ARE OUR JOINED-AT-THE-HIP FRIENDS *and next-door neighbors at Great Waters in Eatonton, Georgia. From Cincinnati, they were wooed to this part of the country by the great golfing opportunities and sunshine. Trim and fit, Karen stays that way by making good food choices. She often prepares this shake-and-serve appetizer, arranging the tomatoes in concentric circles on a large plate.*

Karen's Marinated Cherry Tomatoes

15 to 20 cherry tomatoes
3 tablespoons olive oil
¼ teaspoon garlic salt
½ teaspoon Italian seasonings
Parsley (optional)

Wash tomatoes and place them in a gallon-size plastic zip bag. Add olive oil, garlic salt and Italian seasonings. Shake until well mixed. Refrigerate two to four hours in bag. Arrange on plate with sprigs of parsley. Fifteen to 20 tiny appetizers.

WHEN I WAS A CHILD, MY LUNCH WAS OFTEN A PIMIENTO CHEESE *sandwich with a bowl of chicken noodle soup. The soup came out of the familiar red-and-white-labeled can, and the orange-tinted cheese came out of a small glass with a metal top that you pried off. I didn't know you could get pimiento cheese any other way. When I moved to Georgia, I discovered that people made pimiento cheese and served it as an appetizer. Karen Bain certainly wasn't born a Southern belle, but her recipe for pimiento cheese may qualify her as one. I could eat it by the spoonful.*

Karen's Pimiento Cheese

1 cup shredded cheddar cheese
Small jar (2 ounces) diced pimientos, drained
1 tablespoon green onions, finely chopped
½ tablespoon sugar or no-calorie sweetener, such as Splenda
About ⅓ cup mayonnaise (add more or less to desired consistency)

Mix all ingredients together and chill several hours. Serve with crackers or vegetable crudités, or remove crusts from white bread slices and make small triangle sandwiches. About eight appetizer servings.

JIM'S BROTHER JACK CHRISTENED HIS BOAT "KINSHIP," AND THE *motor vessel has lived up to its name. All of our children and their spouses and some of the grandchildren have cruised on Kinship and celebrated our family ties. One July day with 10 of the Ungerleider gang aboard in Alaskan waters, we baited pots with salmon carcasses and later pulled up a bounty of Dungeness crabs. We gingerly measured each wiggly critter and identified the sex (tossing back the small ones and the females) and then cooked them and removed every bit of shell. It was a family project. Finally, I transformed the crab chunks into dozens of cakes that we polished off in minutes. This recipe is labor-*

intensive if you go to the trouble of catching the crabs; otherwise, it is pretty simple.

Kinship Crab Cakes

$\frac{1}{3}$ cup breadcrumbs (plus additional for
    coating)
1 pound crab meat
1 $\frac{1}{2}$ teaspoons seafood seasoning, such as Old Bay
1 tablespoon fresh lemon juice
$\frac{1}{2}$ teaspoon Worcestershire
$\frac{1}{4}$ cup onion, minced
1 tablespoon garlic, minced
2 tablespoons green bell pepper, minced
2 tablespoons mayonnaise
2 tablespoons fresh parsley, minced

Combine all ingredients and form into nine crab cakes, or more if you want to serve them as appetizers. Roll each patty in additional breadcrumbs. Refrigerate at least one hour.

Spray skillet or griddle with cooking spray (or use butter if you want to be sinful). Cook cakes four minutes per side, or until golden. Serve with Mustard Sauce. Makes three dinner-size servings.

Mustard Sauce
$\frac{1}{2}$ cup mayonnaise
1 tablespoon milk
1 teaspoon Worcestershire
2 tablespoons yellow mustard (or to taste)

Mix all ingredients well and refrigerate at least one hour.

HUMMUS IS THE MOST COMMONLY OFFERED APPETIZER IN DAUGHTER *Jenni's home. It is always homemade. A major ingredient, tahini, is made from sesame seeds and looks like pale peanut butter. Look for it in natural foods stores or in the ethnic section of the grocery.*

Jenni's Hummus

2 cans (16 ounces each) garbanza beans
½ cup tahini paste
3 teaspoons lemon juice
2 cloves garlic, crushed
1 teaspoon Worcestershire sauce
2 tablespoons olive oil
1 tablespoon toasted pine nuts (optional)

Drain beans, reserving some of the water, and place in a blender or food processor. Add tahini, lemon juice, garlic and Worcestershire and blend until smooth. Add some reserved water from beans, if necessary, to make a smooth consistency. Place mixture on a serving dish and drizzle olive oil on top. If you wish, garnish with toasted pine nuts. Serve with pita bread or crisp vegetables, such as carrot sticks, jicama, celery or radishes. Eight to 10 servings.

The Food and Friendship Factor

IT WAS LATE IN THE AFTERNOON ON A WINTER DAY IN THE MID-
1950s. *I was a typical, but timid, young teenager. I brushed my
shoulder-length pageboy, touched up my chin with Clearasil, slipped
into my best dress – a white jersey sheath with a wide matching belt
– and added my favorite necklace, a silver chain with coins dangling
from it.*

*I was heading to the Trinity Baptist Youth Fellowship Christmas
party hosted by the group's advisers, a young married couple. My best
friends would be there – Judy McKenzie and Linda Siders – along
with my latest heartthrob and his pals. There would be music, games
and refreshments.*

*The party began as our advisers distributed Cokes in small green
bottles and guided us to the dining room table, which held baskets of
popcorn and pretzels and a large glass bowl piled high with Mikesell's
potato chips, our hometown brand. The big bowl, which was embossed
with autumn leaves, rested in a gold metallic stand. Attached to its
side was a similar device that held a smaller bowl filled with a creamy
substance. Our hostess said it was a new recipe she thought we would
like – a "dip" for the chips.*

*Curious, we picked up the crisp, salty chips and dipped in. As I
recall, we couldn't get enough of the stuff.*

*That party held over 50 years ago would long be forgotten if it had
not been for my first taste of "California Dip." The recipe, introduced
by Lipton, was a simple combination of sour cream and dried onion
soup mix. It was a hit all over the country.*

*I went home with that recipe in my head, eager to share it with
my mother. It was the first recipe I ever requested – and the beginning
of a lifetime of correlating friendship and food.*

Classic California Dip

> 1 envelope dried onion soup mix, such
>   as Lipton
> 1 pint sour cream (reduced-fat is fine)

Mix the ingredients and chill. Serve with your favorite chips or fresh cut vegetables. About eight servings.

FOOD AND FRIENDSHIP ASSOCIATIONS HAVE PERMEATED MY LIFE. I *remember helping Laura Eblin Fike string steak, mushrooms and onions on dozens of skewers for a backyard cookout, and I recall Jim Stone plopping shrimp in a big pot for a peel-and-eat dinner. I still think about those Friday night TGIF sessions at Barbara Cebuhar's charming home in the Oregon District of Dayton. She welcomed work-weary friends at the door with a glass of red wine and led us to a plate of crackers and this sausage pate.*

Barb's Sausage Pate

3 links hot or mild Italian sausage
1 medium onion, chopped
Italian seasonings to taste
Dash of fennel seeds (optional)
Olive oil or cooking spray
1 package (8 ounces) cream cheese
1 tablespoon Worcestershire sauce
$\frac{1}{4}$ to $\frac{1}{2}$ cup cream or milk
Salt to taste
Parsley (optional)

Remove the casings from the sausage, break it into small pieces and thoroughly brown the meat, onions, Italian seasonings and fennel in a small amount of oil or cooking spray. Put browned ingredients into the bowl of food processor and add cream cheese, Worcestershire and cream or milk. Process until blended. Add salt to taste. Transfer to a small bowl, shape into a ball and chill at least two hours. Turn out onto a plate, garnish with parsley, if you like, and surround with crackers. Eight to 10 servings.

ANITA RICHWINE WAS THE FIRST PERSON TO WELCOME ME WHEN *I joined the staff of the* Kettering-Oakwood Times, *and she has been my loyal friend ever since. We've celebrated career achievements, mourned lost loves and rejoiced over new ones. We've dissected movies and discussed family matters. We've shared countless meals and bottles of wine and carried appetizers like this cheese ball to innumerable parties.*

Anita's Cheese Ball

1 package (8 ounces) cream cheese, at
    room temperature
4 ounces dried beef, chopped
4 green onions, chopped
$\frac{3}{4}$ teaspoon garlic salt
$\frac{3}{4}$ teaspoon flavor enhancement, such as
    Accent (optional)
$\frac{3}{4}$ teaspoon Worcestershire

Mix all ingredients in a medium-sized bowl. Form into a ball. Chill at least two hours. Place on a bed of parsley and surround with crackers. Serve at room temperature. About eight servings.

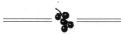

THERE'S ALWAYS ONE HOUSE IN THE NEIGHBORHOOD THAT THE *kids gravitate to. When we lived on Lynnfield Drive in Kettering, Jenni and Greg loved to hang out at the Li home. Susie and Lisa's mother, Anna Li, always had tables full of crafts projects to stimulate the children's creativity and keep their little hands busy. She also introduced the neighborhood to "pot stickers," or Chinese dumplings. Recipes for pot stickers in my cookbooks include ingredients like duck or 'lilybuds' or crawfish. I never got Anna's recipe, but the one I developed uses readily available ingredients just as hers did.*

Pot Stickers Like the Li's

Cooking spray
$\frac{1}{2}$ pound ground pork
2 cloves garlic, minced
1 cup Napa cabbage, finely chopped
1 cup fresh mushrooms, finely chopped
2 green onions, minced
2 teaspoons water chestnuts, minced
1 tablespoon soy sauce
$\frac{1}{2}$ teaspoon salt
1 $\frac{1}{2}$ teaspoons fresh ginger, minced
$\frac{1}{2}$ teaspoon cayenne pepper
1 package wonton wrappers

Spritz a skillet with cooking spray and thoroughly brown ground meat and garlic. Add cabbage, mushrooms, onions and water chestnuts and heat until vegetables soften and meat is well cooked. Add soy sauce, salt, ginger and cayenne and blend well.

Using a small juice glass or biscuit cutter, cut wonton wrappers into circles. Drop a spoonful of the meat mixture onto each wrapper, and fold over into crescent shape, sealing the edges with a bit of water. In a vegetable steamer or bamboo steamer over boiling water, steam the dumplings for eight to 10 minutes. Serve with sauce. (After cooking the pot stickers, you also may fry them in a lightly greased skillet. We prefer them simply steamed.) Makes about 24 pot stickers.

Sauce
2 tablespoons soy sauce
1 teaspoon fresh ginger, minced
$\frac{1}{4}$ teaspoon fresh garlic, minced

Combine soy sauce, ginger and garlic. Chill several hours and serve with the hot pot stickers.

COLD MARGARITAS AND THIS CHILLED APPETIZER ARE A GOOD *summertime combination. Use spinach or dried tomato tortillas for extra color.*

Tortilla Rollups

2 packages (8 ounces each) reduced-fat cream cheese
1 cup reduced-fat sour cream
1 can (4 ounces) chopped green chilies
½ teaspoon garlic powder
6 10-inch tortillas
Salsa for dipping

Combine cream cheese, sour cream, chilies and garlic powder. Divide mixture into six parts and spread each part evenly on a tortilla. Fold in the sides and roll up jelly-roll fashion. Wrap each roll separately in plastic wrap and chill several hours. Cut into one-inch slices. Serve with salsa. Makes about five dozen.

FORTY-SIX YEARS AFTER CLAIMING THEIR SHEEPSKINS FROM *Chaminade in Dayton, six high school buddies and their spouses gathered at our home in Georgia for a mini-reunion. You can imagine the hi-jinks and sports feats relived by the former pigskin and links stars. The group included Tom "Teddy Bear" Geraghty who arrived from Isle of Palms, South Carolina; Dick Kruesch and Bill Westbrock from the Atlanta area; Jack Kenney of Florida, Bill 'Beau' Macbeth, still holding the fort in Dayton, and the party's instigator my husband, Jim "Oogie" Ungerleider. Helen Macbeth*

prepared this dish for one of our many cocktail gatherings.

Helen's Artichoke Crab Spread

1 can (6 ounces) artichokes, drained and
    chopped
1 can (6 ounces) lump crabmeat, drained and
    shredded
1 cup mayonnaise
¼ teaspoon garlic powder
½ cup grated or shredded Parmesan cheese

Mix all ingredients in a bowl. Place in a lightly greased
microwave-safe dish and heat five to seven minutes on
high. Serve with crackers. Eight to 10 servings.

ALTHOUGH WE ARE CONVERTED SOUTHERNERS, JIM AND I HEAD
*north to be with family in Ohio for Christmas, and often we
travel farther north, to Michigan, to be with Dale and Nancy Hines
and Mike and Susan Craig for the New Year holiday. When the air
is frigid, a hot appetizer is welcome at cocktail time. This is one of
Susan's hearty offerings.*

Susan's Appetizer Reubens

1 can (16 ounces) sauerkraut
8 ounces cheddar cheese, shredded
8 ounces Swiss cheese, shredded
¾ cup mayonnaise
4 ounces corned beef, chopped

Mix all ingredients in a bowl and transfer to a lightly
greased quiche-type dish. Heat in a 350-degree
oven for 30 minutes. Serve warm with crackers or
party rye slices. Serves eight to 10.

ROSEMARY AND TERE SEELEY LIVED IN SUBURBAN DAYTON MANY *years just as we did. But it took a move to the South for us to meet and become good friends. Rosemary keeps close ties with old friends. That was apparent when her Dayton book club traveled all the way to Georgia for a meeting. Like the Ya Ya's, they reminisced, partied and managed to fit in some time to discuss the chosen book — on an appropriate topic, women's friendships. This is one of the appetizers Rosemary served the group.*

Rosemary's Sausage Wontons

¾ pound Italian sausage, casings removed
½ cup medium-hot salsa
½ cup Monterey Jack cheese, shredded
1 cup sharp cheddar cheese, shredded
2 ounces diced green chilies
Olive oil or olive-oil-flavored cooking spray
24 wonton skins
Sour cream (optional)
Green onions, sliced (optional)

In a large skillet, brown sausage over medium heat, breaking it up with a fork. Remove with slotted spoon and place meat on paper towels, squeezing to remove as much grease as possible. Drain drippings from pan. Return sausage to the skillet, add salsa, cheeses and green chilies. Simmer until mixture thickens, about five minutes. Remove from heat and cool to room temperature.

Brush mini-muffin pans with olive oil or spray. Press one wonton wrapper into each muffin cup. Fill each wrapper with a generous tablespoon of the cooled meat-cheese mixture. (Up to this point, this recipe can be prepared up to 24 hours in advance. Cover and refrigerate.)

Bake at 350 degrees five to 10 minutes, until edges start to brown. Transfer wonton from muffin cups to baking sheet. Bake until bottoms are crisp, about 10 minutes longer. Transfer to serving platter. If desired, garnish with sour cream and green onions. Makes 24 appetizers.

ROSEMARY ALSO IS A VITAL MEMBER OF A BOOK CLUB AT REYNOLDS *Plantation that includes Joan Miles, Peg Trowbridge, Cheryl Taylor and me. Generally, our husbands celebrate BNO (boys' night out) monthly while we women meet. Sometimes we mingle with the "boys" as we did one evening when Cheryl entertained us south-of-the-border style. Dave Taylor mixed margaritas as Cheryl set out this bean and cheese appetizer. This Mexican dip is partially layered and then baked a short time before it is topped with the remaining cold ingredients. We all requested the recipe.*

Cheryl's Seven-Layer Dip

1 can (16 ounces) refried beans
1 tablespoon taco seasoning
1 cup shredded cheddar or Monterey Jack
   cheese, or both
⅓ cup black olives, sliced, pitted and drained
1 large tomato, chopped
1 cup sour cream
1 cup guacamole
1 cup salsa
Tortilla chips

Mix the taco seasoning into the refried beans. Spread the combination into a lightly greased 10-inch glass pie plate or baking dish. Spread the cheese on top; then sprinkle the olives on top of the cheese layer. Place the baking dish in a preheated 350-degree oven for 12 minutes, or until the cheese melts and bubbles up. Finally, sprinkle the tomato evenly over the top, next layer the sour cream, then the guacamole, and top with salsa. Serve immediately. Serves 10.

JOE AND JOYCE ANDERSON SURFACED AS OUR NEW BEST FRIENDS *when Jim and I left our Georgia retirement home and moved temporarily to the Ohio River Valley. When Jim joined Holzer Clinic and Holzer Medical Center to head up the cancer program, he quickly discovered that Joe, an internist, shared our fervor for boating and our enjoyment of good music.*

Joyce and Joe introduced us to the Ohio Valley Symphony. We were astonished to find that a town as small as Gallipolis (fewer than 5,000 residents) was home to an honest-to-goodness professional symphony. We were even more surprised when we heard the beautiful music resounding in the restored Ariel Theatre.

Joyce serves as the organization's treasurer and is involved in raising funds to keep the symphony afloat. This is one of her recipes served at a reception for symphony supporters. Make it the day before you plan to serve it.

Joyce's Shrimp Mold

1 can (15 ounces) condensed tomato soup
3 packages (3 ounces each) cream cheese
2 tablespoons unflavored gelatin
½ cup cold water
1 cup mayonnaise (not salad dressing)
¼ cup green pepper, finely chopped
1 small onion, finely chopped (about ⅓ cup)
1 pound small frozen cooked shrimp, thawed

Place soup in medium saucepan and bring to boil. Remove from heat and add cheese. Beat with electric mixer until smooth. Dissolve gelatin in cold water. Add to tomato mixture, stir and cool. When cooled, add mayonnaise, green pepper, onion and shrimp. Pour into a lightly greased ring mold or medium-sized bowl and chill overnight. Unmold onto a bed of parsley or lettuce and serve with crackers. Serves eight to 10.

Beverages

J IM DRINKS DIRTY MARTINI'S AND HE'S FUSSY ABOUT THE *preparation. He and my father, had they met, would have gotten along well; martini's were Daddy's cocktail choice too. It is said that when prohibition ended, FDR served these drinks to his guests in the White House. The President's martini, however, included some vermouth. Jim's is simply gin and olive juice – and a couple of olives. He even has a pronged instrument to pluck the olives from the jar. The juice gets fuzzy looking if you stick your fingers in it. Designate a driver if you drink one of these.*

Jim's Dirty Martini

3 ounces good-quality gin, such as Beefeater
1 to 3 teaspoons olive juice, to taste
2 queen-size pimiento-stuffed olives

Place a few ice cubes in a cocktail shaker. Measure three ounces of gin and pour over the ice. Add olive juice. Place two olives in the martini glass. Shake the gin, olive juice and ice cubes three or four times, and let it sit a moment to chill. Strain and pour over the olives. One generous serving. Cheers!

MARTINI'S NEVER APPEALED TO ME UNTIL I SAW A WOMAN *holding a pale green cocktail in an elegant martini glass. I told the bartender I wanted to sample what she was drinking. He served the drink with a paper-thin slice of apple floating on the liquid. One sip of the sweet-tart flavor and I was a convert. One is my limit and Jim never fails to say, "Goodnight, Joan," when he serves it to me.*

Joan's Apple Martini

1 ½ ounces apple schnapps, such as Sour Apple
  Pucker
2 ounces vodka
Half apple slice or maraschino cherry (optional)

Place a few ice cubes in a cocktail shaker and pour apple schnapps and vodka over them. Shake a couple of times and let the mixture sit a minute to chill. Strain and pour into a martini glass and float a very thin half slice of apple on top, or serve with a maraschino cherry. One serving.

MY PETITE, UNDERWEIGHT MOTHER PIGGED OUT ON CANDY AND *indulged in rich desserts, but she was prudent about consuming alcohol. When she agreed to have a cocktail, at the prodding of my father, she chose a whiskey sour. Daddy pulled out his silver-plated shaker, shook the ingredients just so, and dropped a slice of orange and a long-stemmed cherry into the glass before he poured the drink. Daddy had a penchant for barware so we had glasses used exclusively for various trendy drinks – wide-mouthed martini glasses, squat glassware to hold an old-fashioned, snifters for brandy and the slender glasses made especially for Mother's whiskey sours.*

Mother's Whiskey Sour

Juice of ½ lemon
2 teaspoons confectioner's sugar
2 ounces bourbon
Half orange slice
Long-stemmed maraschino cherry

Place ice cubes in shaker. Add lemon juice, sugar and bourbon and shake well. Strain and pour over an orange slice and cherry in the glass. One serving.

G UESTS WHO CAME TO MY OAKWOOD HOME KNEW MY BARTENDING *skills were limited. I had two specialties: blender daiquiri's for hot summer days and hot buttered rum in the winter. For the hot rum drinks, I bought a mix and followed the directions. My frosty daiquiri recipe is super easy.*

Blender Daiquiri's

1 can (12 ounces) frozen limeade concentrate
12 ounces rum
12 to 15 ice cubes

Place frozen concentrate, rum and ice cubes in blender container. Put the lid on. Blend on high until drink is slushy. Serve immediately in wine glasses. Six servings.

O N OUR FIRST VACATION IN FLORIDA TOGETHER, JIM AND I SET OUT *to find a casual beachside restaurant for a late breakfast. We spotted a weathered building on stilts that displayed an "Open for Breakfast' sign. A waiter greeted us and led us to a balcony where*

he presented us with two champagne glasses and a frosty pitcher of juice. I think he winked at Jim as I appreciatively sipped the chilled beverage. The day was breezy, and down below, as if on cue, a panorama of surfers appeared in colorful wetsuits. We lingered for hours, watching them gracefully ride the giant rolling waves. I'm sure we ate breakfast at some point, but all I remember is the magic of the moment and the mimosas.

Vacation Mimosas

Champagne
Orange juice

Mix equal amounts in a clear glass pitcher and serve in champagne glasses.

T*RY* 18 *HOLES OF GOLF ON A MUGGY DAY IN* G*EORGIA, AND YOU return to the house with skin drenched and throats parched. On one such day, Jim offered a choice of lemonade or beer to our guests, Nancy and Bob Westfall from Bellbrook, Ohio. Nancy said, "I'd like a shandy."*

Jim had no idea what she meant. "I'll make it," she added. She proceeded to pour half a glass of lemonade and poured an equal amount of beer on top and then stirred it. "That's a shandy," she said.

It was the best thirst quencher I've ever had. Nancy first sampled the drink in England when she visited her daughter. Apparently, the beverage is centuries old and was drunk on hot days by African hunters.

Nancy's Shandy

½ glass cold beer
½ glass cold lemonade (sugar-free type, such
   as Crystal Light, is fine)

Combine beer and lemonade and stir. This drink is especially appealing served in a Pilsner glass.

THERE'S A SPECIAL BOND AMONG SINGLE MOTHERS RAISING *children. Carole Helminiak and Joanne Carr became my soul sisters when we three experienced divorce and lived in Oakwood. Each of us had two small children and lived on tight budgets, but one winter we squirreled away enough money for a brief road trip to Florida and sweet-talked our exes into caring for the kids for four days.*

On the trip, we economized by dining on hamburgers at McDonald's, then retreating to a luxurious hotel for an expensive nightcap. My splurge was a Brandy Alexander made with ice cream.

Brandy Alexander with Ice Cream

4 ounces brandy
2 ounces crème de cacao
3 cups vanilla ice cream
Nutmeg

Place brandy, crème de cacao and ice cream in a blender; process until smooth. Spoon into martini glasses or other stemmed glasses. Dust with nutmeg. Four servings.

FORMER SISTER-IN-LAW PENNY DARCY INTRODUCED ME TO THIS *tall non-alcoholic beverage in Palm Springs. Out West, they call it an "Arnie Palmer." In our part of Georgia, they call the combination "Gentleman Jim's." I make the lemonade from a sugar-free mix so the drink has no calories.*

Arnie Palmer (Gentleman Jim's)

Half glass iced tea
Half glass lemonade
Dash cinnamon (optional)

Dash ground cloves (optional)

Mix all the ingredients together and pour over ice. Garnish with a slice of lemon or a sprig of mint. One serving.

Mother's Days

MOTHER'S CULINARY PRACTICES EPITOMIZED THE AD SLOGAN, *"Nothin' says lovin' like somethin' from the oven." My conventional stay-at-home mother fulfilled her need for accomplishment by baking cakes and other sweets. She gave testimony to her love by sharing her kitchen with me at an early age.*

In our matching red-and-white gingham aprons, we cracked eggs together, and with our index fingers coaxed every trace of slippery white into the mixing bowl. Under her direction, I sifted and stirred and we tasted and marveled at the texture of our creations.

Mother was a slight woman, who, by drinking thick malts and eating quantities of candy, kept her weight up to 100 pounds. She had heavy dark hair and deep brown eyes and was proud that someone once told her she looked like actress Ida Lupino.

Her patience was unlimited as we cooked. When I was mature enough to be trusted at the gas stove, she taught me to make cream puffs. Making these pastries was a highly sensory experience. As I combined the eggs and flour, she advised me. "You'll know when the batter is ready; it will look velvety." And magically, at a given moment, the mixture developed a distinctive sheen. Then I moved on to the next steps—baking the puffs, slitting off the crusty caps and scooping out the moist filament to make room for the filling.

Our filling was always Jello pudding. We varied the flavors; sometimes chocolate was the choice; other days, lemon or vanilla. She always let me choose. We spooned the filling into the pastry vessels, replaced the tops and dusted them with powdered sugar. Then we arranged them on a round platter and stood back to admire our handiwork.

A SHY, MODEST WOMAN, MOTHER KEPT TO HERSELF AND *restricted her outings to occasional visits with family and close friends, with me, her only child, in tow. Despite my urgings, she would not attend PTA meetings like the other mothers but she obligingly paid membership dues and responded to all requests. One time she prepared an applesauce cake for the PTA bake sale and beamed when she heard it was the first item sold.*

When I was nine years old, that same recipe earned me recognition. We were city people and our only acquaintance with agriculture was our annual excursion to the Montgomery County Fair. Every spring when I got my final report card at Jefferson Elementary School, I looked for the discount admission coupons that were always tucked inside. I put them in a safe place and at the end of summer, Mother – who never learned to drive – and I rode the Lexington Avenue trolley downtown and then transferred to the bus that took us to the fairgrounds.

Besides Christmas, this was my favorite day of the year. First we went to the cow barn to see milking demonstrations; then we watched farmers shear swaths of wool from accommodating sheep. We held our noses as we wandered by the pigs and gawked at fancy roosters and flop-eared rabbits.

Finally we ventured into the coliseum to see the crafts and cooking displays. Mother admired the stitchery. I liked to look at the food – giant pumpkins and cabbages, homemade jams in jars trimmed with checkered and plaid fabrics, overstuffed pies and multi-layered tortes.

One year we picked up an application to compete with the rural families who dominated the fair. I kept that form all year in my underwear drawer, and the next summer, I prepared Mother's applesauce cake, generously lathering it with cream cheese frosting with specks of orange peel in it. On the appointed day, we rode the trolley to deliver my entry, and a day later, we returned to the fairgrounds. This time, our first stop was the high-domed coliseum where we hurried up the broad wooden staircase to find the display of pastries.

We spotted the cake immediately — it was up front, and there propped next to it was a ribbon. It was a red one — not blue — but there never could have been two more victorious people.

I often think about Mother, a sweet woman who filled her days by sharing simple joys with me. Whenever that plump Pillsbury doughboy appears on my television screen, I see him wink at me, and I can almost hear him whisper, "It's time to turn the oven on."

Desserts

Mother's small aluminum angel food cake pan was *battered and bent from frequent use. We just piled on extra frosting to cover the resulting imperfections in the cake. Note that you must use a small-sized angel food pan for this recipe. The cake is best if you make it the day before serving it. Store it in the refrigerator overnight, but bring it to room temperature to serve.*

Mother's Prize Applesauce Cake

1 ⅔ cups flour
1 ⅓ cups sugar
¼ teaspoon baking powder
1 teaspoon baking soda
¾ teaspoon salt
½ teaspoon cinnamon
¼ teaspoon cloves
¼ teaspoon allspice
⅓ cup softened shortening, such as Crisco
⅓ cup water
⅓ cup chopped walnuts
⅔ cup raisins
1 cup unsweetened applesauce
1 large egg

Sift dry ingredients together. Add shortening, water, nuts, raisins and applesauce and beat vigorously with spoon for two minutes (or mix with electric mixer on low for two minutes). Scrape bowl frequently. Add egg. Beat two more minutes, scraping bowl often. Pour batter into lightly greased small angel food cake pan. Bake 50 to 55 minutes at 350 degrees or until tester comes out clean. Cool completely. Remove from pan and frost with Creamy Orange Icing. Serves eight.

Creamy Orange Icing

1 package (8 ounces) cream cheese at
    room temperature
2 tablespoons butter at room temperature
1 pound confectioner's sugar
Grated peel from one large orange
Juice from one large orange

With an electric mixer, combine cream cheese, butter and confectioner's sugar, adding orange peel and enough orange juice to make the icing a spreading consistency.

MY MOTHER TOOK A FEW COMMON INGREDIENTS AND TRANSFORMED them into an endless variety of delicacies. Cream puffs were an example. This pastry, sometimes referred to as "pate a choux" is versatile. "Choux" means cabbage in French, and the puffs resemble little cabbages when they rise. The pastry is also suitable for appetizers; just drop by teaspoons into 12 puffs and fill with cheese spreads, chicken salad or a mixture of your choice. This recipe makes six dessert-sized puffs.

Mother's Cream Puffs

$\frac{1}{2}$ cup water
$\frac{1}{4}$ cup butter (use the real thing)
$\frac{1}{2}$ cup flour
2 eggs
2 cups prepared pudding
Confectioner's sugar

Preheat oven to 400 degrees. In a small saucepan, heat water and butter to boiling point.

Add flour and stir constantly until mixture leaves

sides of pan and forms a ball. Remove from heat. Cool. With a spoon, beat in two eggs, one at a time, until mixture is smooth. Drop from a tablespoon into six mounds placed three inches apart on a lightly greased baking sheet. Bake 30 minutes at 400 degrees. When baked, allow puffs to cool. Cut off tops, scooping out filaments of soft dough with a spoon. Fill puffs with pudding, replace tops and dust with confectioner's sugar. Serves six.

O N OUR MONTGOMERY COUNTY FAIR FORAYS, MOTHER AND I *shared a big crunchy waffle loaded with powdered sugar. At home, we made small replicas. Cookbooks refer to these pastries as patty shells or rosettes, but we called them "fair waffles." You need a rosette iron to make these; kitchenware shops often stock them in butterfly and snowflake shapes. Be sure you have a deep-fat thermometer on hand too.*

Mother's County Fair Waffles

1 cup flour
1 cup milk
½ teaspoon salt
2 teaspoons sugar
1 egg
Vegetable oil for frying
Confectioner's sugar

Using an electric mixer, beat flour, milk, salt, sugar and egg into a smooth batter.

Pour oil to a depth of about three inches in a medium-sized saucepan. Heat oil to 365 degrees. Dip iron into oil to heat it and then quickly into batter, taking care to cover only the bottom and sides of the form with the batter. Quickly lower the batter-covered iron into the oil until the shell begins to brown and pull away from the sides. Use a fork to ease the shell away from the iron. Don't despair; it may take a few tries to perfect the technique. With tongs, lift the lightly browned shell from the oil and place on paper towels to drain. From time to time, as you are frying the waffles, remove errant pieces of pastry from the oil with a slotted spoon. When waffles are cool, put about a half cup of confectioner's sugar in a sieve and powder the tops. Makes about three dozen, depending on the size of your iron. You can store these a few days in an airtight container.

A HEAVY OLD IRON SKILLET WAS MOTHER'S MOST FREQUENTLY *used cooking utensil. She fried bacon, simmered spaghetti sauce and made cakes in the skillet. She apparently knew this recipe by heart; I never found it in writing. I've fabricated this one by combining elements from several recipes in my cookbooks. It tastes like the cake I remember. When you make it, let the children place the pineapple rings and cherries in the skillet. They will be pleased with the pattern when you turn the cake over on a platter. If you don't have an iron skillet, use a nine or 10-inch pan that is safe on the stovetop and in the oven.*

Mother's Pineapple Upside Down Cake

1 stick margarine
1½ cups light brown sugar, packed
1 can (15 ounces) pineapple slices (reserve the juice)
7 maraschino cherries (without stems)
¾ cup sugar
4 tablespoons shortening, such as Crisco
2 eggs
1½ cups flour

$\frac{1}{2}$ teaspoon salt
1 teaspoon vanilla
2 teaspoons baking powder
$\frac{1}{4}$ teaspoon baking soda
$\frac{1}{2}$ cup reserved pineapple juice

Melt margarine over low heat in a nine to 10-inch ovenproof skillet or metal baking pan. Add brown sugar and stir over low heat until caramelized. Place seven pineapple slices over the mixture and place a cherry in the center of each ring.

In a large bowl, cream the sugar and shortening. Add the eggs, flour, salt, vanilla, baking powder, baking soda and pineapple juice. Mix well. Pour the batter slowly over the pineapple and sugar mixture in the pan. Bake in a preheated 350-degree oven for 35 to 45 minutes or until a pick comes out clean. Cool 10 minutes. Then put large plate over the skillet and flip quickly. Eight to 10 servings.

G RANDMA, LIKE OTHER GOOD COOKS OF HER VINTAGE, INITIALLY *used lard to make pastry, but she eventually embraced Crisco, which, incidentally, was introduced to the public in 1911. One day in 1991, she called to tell me her latest discovery: Crisco was available in sticks. Both of us switched to the new style, packaged for easy measuring. I know you'll tell me that it's more convenient to simply buy refrigerated prepared crusts. But at least once, give this recipe a try and do a taste comparison.*

Grandma's Pie Crust

$2\frac{1}{4}$ cups flour
1 teaspoon salt
$\frac{1}{4}$ cup water

¾ cup shortening, such as Crisco

Sift flour and salt together. Stir. Remove one-half cup of the flour-salt mixture and add ¼ cup water to it. Stir until smooth. Cut the shortening into the remaining flour with a pastry blender until the pieces are the size of small peas. Add the flour-salt paste to the flour mixture and mix until a ball is formed. Divide into two pieces and roll out on a floured board. Makes crusts for two 9-inch pies.

O N THANKSGIVING, GRANDMA PRESENTED HER PUMPKIN PIE AS IF *it were a crown on a velvet pillow. She lapped up our ooh's and ah's as she brought the oversized dessert to the table. She baked pies in a glass dish that measured 11 inches from rim to rim. Grandma also distinguished her pie by grating nutmeg on top before she baked it. It had to be freshly grated – none of the ground powder in a tin for her. These measurements will make the more common nine-inch pie.*

Grandma's Pumpkin Pie

1 can (15 ounces) pumpkin
½ cup dark brown sugar
½ cup granulated sugar
½ teaspoon salt
1 tablespoon flour
1 teaspoon cinnamon
¼ teaspoon ground cloves
¼ teaspoon ground ginger
2 eggs, slightly beaten
1 cup whole milk
Nutmeg
Unbaked pie crust

Preheat oven to 425 degrees. In a large bowl,

thoroughly mix pumpkin, sugars, salt, flour, and spices. Add eggs and milk and stir until combined. Pour into a nine-inch unbaked piecrust. Grate fresh nutmeg evenly over top of pie. Bake for 45 to 50 minutes, or until knife inserted comes out clean. Six to eight servings.

B Y THE TIME HE WAS FOUR YEARS OLD, MY SON GREG HAD A FIRMLY *developed set of family values. One day we were having lunch in a family-style restaurant and after we polished off our meal, the waitress turned to Greg and asked, "Would you like a piece of pie for dessert?" The preschooler innocently inquired, "Do you make your pies from scrap here?" We couldn't repress our giggles.*

Greg is fortunate that he married a woman who prefers homemade pies too. Carrie capably has assumed Grandma's role in baking the tastiest pie of all — strawberry-rhubarb. Carrie makes hers with a lattice top just as Grandma did.

Carrie and Grandma's Strawberry-Rhubarb Pie

2 cups sugar
⅔ cup flour
1 egg, slightly beaten
3 cups fresh rhubarb, sliced (if you use frozen, thaw and drain)
3 cups fresh strawberries, sliced (thaw and drain if frozen)
1 tablespoon butter
Pastry for double crust

Preheat oven to 425 degrees. Combine sugar and flour in a large bowl. Add egg, rhubarb and strawberries and stir well. Spoon into a pastry-lined pie dish and dot with butter. Cover with lattice crust. Bake about 55 minutes or until crust is brown and juices are bubbling. Put a cookie sheet on the shelf below the pie while it is baking so it doesn't drip on your oven. Six to eight servings.

ACONFESSION; I HAVE NEVER PREPARED THIS RECIPE. THE *"mincemeat" in my Thanksgiving pies comes from a jar and has no meat content. I pass on this recipe for historical interest. I can't imagine anyone going to all this trouble for a dessert. If you do make it, please let me know how it turns out. Grandma, incidentally, used a hand grinder. Nothing made my Grandpa Schillo happier than eating a serving of this pie, warm with vanilla ice cream on top. This makes a lot, and you will need a large pan to mix it.*

Grandma's Labor-Intensive Mincemeat

1 ½ pounds lean beef chunks
1 pound suet
7 pounds apples, pared and seeded
½ pound citron
2 pounds raisins
1 pound currants
6 oranges
3 lemons
2 pounds sugar
½ gallon apple cider
3 teaspoons each cinnamon, nutmeg, allspice

Cook beef in water until done (about 40 minutes). Cool. Grind the beef. Grind the suet (but do not cook it). Chop the citron. Chop or coarsely grind the apples. Remove seeds from oranges and lemons and coarsely grind the fruit and the peeling. Combine sugar and cider and add the apples, citron, raisins, currants, oranges, lemons and spices. Heat on medium for 20 minutes, stirring so mixture doesn't burn. Add beef and suet. Mix well and place in sterilized quart canning jars. Process according to canning directions. Makes six or seven quarts, enough for six or seven pies.

To make one pie, you will need two unbaked pie crusts and one quart mincemeat. Line a nine-inch pie plate with pastry. Fill with mincemeat. Put top crust on and seal and crimp edges. Cut slits in top. Bake at 400 degrees for 35 to 40 minutes. Serves six to eight.

MOTHER'S SISTER AND BROTHER-IN-LAW, THELMA AND JOHN *Kubilius, lived on Deeds Avenue when I was in first grade. Mother and I would walk hand-in-hand from our house on Notre Dame Avenue to have lunch with Aunt Thelma and my cousin Nancy. Their old house with its stained glass window and pocket doors fascinated me.*

I loved the way Aunt Thelma laughed; she laughed more than anyone else in our family. I was envious when Nancy got a baby brother; they named him Randy. It's hard to believe that Nancy is a grandmother now, and Randy is retired. In her 80s, Aunt Thelma still tells jokes and giggles the way she did years ago. This is one of her specialty desserts.

Aunt Thelma's Peanut Butter Pie

1 baked 9-inch pie shell
$\frac{1}{2}$ cup confectioner's sugar
3 heaping tablespoons peanut butter
2 boxes (3 ounces each) cook-and-serve vanilla
    pudding mix
$3\frac{1}{2}$ cups milk

Additional 3 heaping tablespoons peanut butter
Whipped cream or whipped topping,
    such as Cool Whip

In a small bowl, thoroughly mix sugar and peanut butter. Sprinkle half this mixture on top of baked pie shell. Reserve the rest. In a large saucepan, mix milk and pudding mix and cook as directed on the package. Just before removing from the heat, add three heaping tablespoons peanut butter. Stir until blended. Cool the mixture.

Pour cooled mixture into crust. Refrigerate two to three hours. Cover pie with whipped cream. Sprinkle remaining sugar-peanut butter mixture over the top. Serves six to eight.

Cultivating Chi Omegas

MRS. O.U. TERRILL WAS ABOVE REPROACH IN ALL RESPECTS. A *genteel, shriveled Southern lady, educated by a governess, she lived with some 60 young women with strong personalities and active hormones in the Chi Omega house at Ohio University. In local bars, we sorority girls chugged our beers and belted out current songs. But when we were with our housemother, we met her expectations of propriety.*

Mrs. Terrilll's rules included "dressing" for dinner — no scruffy shoes, no jeans, not even slacks. Skirts were required dinner wear. Each evening, we lined up in the hallway and waited for her to lead us into the dining room. We did not lift our forks until she signaled. She used a little bell to summon the busboys, who we surreptitiously eyed. But we never exchanged a word with them, even if we had a date with one an hour later. It would not be considered proper to socialize with the busboys during dinner.

The meals we ate at the sorority house were undistinguished — tuna noodle casserole, fried chicken, fruit plates with chicken salad and muffins. But one menu item captured my attention and appreciation. It was totally new to me – chess pie.

Mrs. Terrill had provided our sorority's cook with her own personal recipe. I regret that I moved from that house without getting a copy of it. Chess pie is a distinctively Southern dessert, one that resonates purity and refinement – the imprint that this patient lady endeavored to leave on her collegiate charges.

FORTY YEARS PASSED SINCE I ATE THAT DESSERT, AND THEN ONE *day at my weekly writers' gathering in Greensboro, Georgia, I read this remembrance of Mrs. Terrill and chess pie. One woman, Alabama-born Kathy Wright, listened intently as I spoke.*

Little did I suspect what she had in store for me. I was unable to attend the following week's writers' session, and she expressed her disappointment in a note a few days later.

"Dear Joan, I made two chess pies for the writing group and you weren't there! I wanted to make them especially for you after your last story. I'm sorry you missed eating them with us."

I was awash with the warmth of her gesture and immediately took out my pie pan and prepared the recipe she had enclosed with the note. That first bite was a commemorative moment.

Just as I remember Mrs. Terrill as the embodiment of Southern hospitality – so, too, will I remember Kathy.

When you make this pie, do not be dismayed that it contains vinegar and cornmeal. I can almost guarantee that you will like it.

Kathy's Chess Pie

1 stick margarine, melted
3 eggs
1 ½ cups sugar
2 tablespoons vinegar
1 ½ tablespoons cornmeal
1 teaspoon vanilla
1 8-inch unbaked deep-dish pie shell

Preheat oven to 425 degrees. Blend melted margarine with eggs, sugar, vinegar, cornmeal and vanilla. Pour mixture into unbaked pie shell. Put pie into oven on lowest rack. Immediately lower temperature to 350 degrees and bake about 50 minutes or longer, until filling is firm.

If crust starts getting too brown during baking, cover edges with foil. Six to eight servings.

ONE DAY I DELIVERED A COUPLE OF PIECES OF KATHY'S CHESS PIE TO *neighbors Ethelene and Norm Slucher. A few days later, Ethelene, a Kentucky native, sent a whole pie to our house. It was her version of chess pie, this one made with buttermilk. We ate the first pieces while the pie was still warm, and the rest didn't last long. Ethelene never makes one pie, but always two, so she has one to share.*

Ethelene's Buttermilk Pie

1 stick margarine, softened
2 cups sugar (or no-calorie sweetener, such as Splenda)
2 tablespoons flour
4 eggs
1 teaspoon vanilla
⅔ cup buttermilk
9-inch deep-dish frozen pie shell

Using a mixer, cream the margarine, sugar and flour. Add eggs, one at a time. Add vanilla and buttermilk and mix. Pour into pie shell. Bake at 350 degrees about 45 minutes, until slightly browned and an inserted knife comes out clean. Serves six to eight.

THE GREENSBORO WRITERS' GUILD IS A DIVERSE BUNCH OF PEOPLE *united by a passion for writing. Members meet faithfully every Tuesday afternoon.*

One member surprised us when she announced she would be away for an extended period. Jenny Watkins said she was following her heart to the Pacific Crest Trail. There, she would cover more than 2,500 miles on foot from Mexico to Canada. The goal was inconceivable to us, and we were awed by her perseverance as she e-mailed us periodically from the trail. Months later, we celebrated her return with respect for her achievement.

It was accomplished through great discipline, which she exerted in other aspects of her life, such as eating. Although she did eat meat to provide stamina on her hike, Jenny was a raw foods advocate. One day she came to the meeting with a pie in hand. She explained that it was a raw pie, and we reacted as you might expect. However, it was good – and nutritious.

If you want a new food experience, try making this sweet potato dessert. I made the pie for a Thanksgiving dinner, and son Jason ate at least half of it. Of course, he piled whipped cream on top. I'm not sure Jenny would have approved.

Jenny's Raw Sweet Potato Pie

Crust
1 ½ cups almonds
1 cup dates
1 to 2 tablespoons orange juice

In a food processor, chop nuts until finely ground. Add dates and process until finely ground. Add orange juice to moisten. Press mixture into a nine-inch pie plate.

Filling
2 medium-sized sweet potatoes
10 large pitted Medjool dates, or other large dates
½ teaspoon allspice

$\frac{1}{2}$ teaspoon cinnamon
1 tablespoon vanilla
1 teaspoon fresh ginger, chopped fine
$\frac{1}{2}$ cup walnuts or almonds, chopped,
for topping

Wash and peel potatoes and cut into chunks. Place in processor with the pitted dates and process until smooth (it will take some time to make it smooth and fine). Add spices and vanilla and process until well blended. Spoon filling into the crust and sprinkle evenly with chopped nuts. Refrigerate at least one hour before serving. Serves six to eight.

A FFABLE GORDIE NORTH IS A FREQUENT GOLFING PARTNER OF JIM'S. *He lives in Georgia most of the winter, but spends his summers at his Michigan home. One evening he appeared unannounced on our porch with a pie in hand — one that he made himself. It was banana cream — and Jim declared it was his favorite pie, something I had not learned in our more than 10 years of marriage. Gordie gave some guidance and now Jim can whip up a pie in a jiffy, using prepared crust and pudding mix. Gordie brought the pie in a disposable foil pie pan with a plastic cover. These are handy to keep in the pantry for delivering pies to your friends.*

Gordie (and Jim's) Quick Banana Cream Pie

1 package (3$\frac{1}{2}$ ounces) vanilla pudding mix
2 cups milk
1 prepared graham cracker crumb crust
About 2 cups whipped topping, such as
Cool Whip
1 large banana, sliced

Prepare pudding according to directions for pie on package. Line prepared crust with banana slices. Pour pudding over slices. Frost with whipped topping. Serves six.

SUZANNE AND TOM GERAGHTY, WHO GREW UP IN DAYTON, RETIRED *to a new home at Isle of Palms, South Carolina. Their visitors are treated to a water view when they awake in the guest room and to good homemade food throughout the day. This is one of Suzanne's favorite pies; it was a specialty of her former mother-in-law Evangeline. The old-fashioned filling is satisfying and not so sweet as banana pies prepared with pudding mix.*

Evangeline's Banana Cream Pie

2 egg yolks (save the whites for meringue
    if you wish)
1 ½ cups milk
4 tablespoons butter
6 tablespoons flour
½ cup sugar
1 teaspoon vanilla
2 ripe bananas, sliced
9-inch baked pie shell
Whipped topping, such as Cool Whip
    (or meringue)

Mix egg yolks and milk and set aside. Melt butter in a small saucepan and add flour and sugar. Stir. Add egg-milk mixture to pan and stir and cook over medium heat until it thickens. Remove from heat and add vanilla. Cool slightly. Spoon half the mixture into the baked pie shell and place most of the bananas on top. Cover with remaining cream mixture. Top with whipped topping or with meringue if you prefer. Garnish with remaining banana slices. Chill before serving. Serves six.

Jim's son Jason spent his early career years "batching it" in San Francisco and New York City so we did not get to see him as often as the Ohio-based offspring. On one of his brief visits to our home in Worthington, Ohio, the three of us tackled the art of pasta-making. By the time we finished, the kitchen counters were gluey and the floor dusted with flour, but we had a great time – sharing movie reviews, joking about childhood memories and discussing life's turns. From my perspective, conversations in the kitchen are among the most meaningful forms of communication, and I realized I had gotten to know Jason much better that day.

While he appreciates good food, Jason doesn't have much of a reputation for cooking so he surprised us one Thanksgiving Day when he proffered a homemade pie. We heeded his advice to serve it to adults only. It was heavily spiked with bourbon. The recipe below is more conservatively flavored than his original.

I've always used light Karo syrup for my pecan pies, but didn't know what to do with the leftover syrup. Should I put it in the refrigerator? If so, how long will it stay good? I took a look at the Karo website, which is worth visiting, and learned that it keeps indefinitely and does not need to be refrigerated. The website has recipes for 27 kinds of pecan pie, ranging from Frozen Butter Pecan Pie to Cheesecake Pecan Pie. This pie is similar to Karo's Bourbon Pecan Pie, but packs a little more punch.

Jason's Pecan Pie for Adults

6 tablespoons butter, softened
1 cup dark brown sugar
4 eggs, slightly beaten
1 teaspoon vanilla
¾ cup light corn syrup, such as Karo
¼ cup bourbon

2 cups pecan halves
1 9-inch unbaked pie crust

With an electric mixer, cream butter and brown sugar in a medium bowl. Add eggs, vanilla, corn syrup and bourbon. Mix well at low speed. Fold in the pecans. Pour mixture into the pastry. Bake at 350 degrees 55 to 60 minutes, or until filling in center is almost set. Cool on wire rack. Serves six to eight.

JIM ASSERTS THAT HIS MOTHER FLORENCE'S CHEESECAKE IS THE BEST *ever. She served it at Sully's, the Ungerleiders' restaurant on Salem Avenue in Dayton View. Jim remembers that customers would check on the cake's availability before placing reservations.*

Florence's cousin Charlie Cooper preserved the recipe and handed it down to us. It produces a big cake – and it's tricky to make. The first time I baked it, Jim complained it didn't have a hole in the middle! The recipe did not specify using an angel food cake pan. The second time I made it, I apparently didn't allow enough baking time for the deep pan, and we resorted to eating it with a spoon. Then we chose it as our wedding cake. I baked it and served it to our family on the day of our marriage, October 15, 1994. I got it right this time. Jim said Florence would approve of his bride.

Sully's Cheesecake

Crust
1 package (6 ounces) zwieback (look in the baby food section of the grocery; if you can't find it, substitute graham cracker crumbs, about 1½ cups)
1 cup sugar
1 teaspoon cinnamon
½ cup butter, melted

Roll zwieback fine in a plastic bag (or pulverize it in a blender). Hand mix with sugar, cinnamon and melted butter. Set aside ¾ cup of the mixture to sprinkle on top of the cake. Grease a large angel food cake pan. Spread and press zwieback mixture on bottom and sides.

Filling

5 packages (8 ounces each) cream cheese
   (yes, five packages!)
1½ cups sugar
6 eggs
1/8 teaspoon salt
Grated rind and juice from 1 large lemon
½ cup flour
1 teaspoon vanilla
1½ cups whipping cream

With an electric mixer, beat cheese, sugar, eggs and salt on high speed until light in color. Add lemon juice, grated rind, flour and vanilla and beat. In a separate bowl, beat whipping cream until it makes soft peaks. Fold into cheese mixture Put into prepared pan. Sprinkle remaining zwieback mixture over top. Put in a preheated 350-degree oven about 70 to 75 minutes or until set. Turn off heat, open oven door, and let stand in oven one hour longer or until cool. Twelve to 14 servings.

FOR YEARS, GRANDMA TOOK CREDIT FOR THIS CREAMY CAKE. BUT *now the truth must be told. In 1963, when I was the food writer for the Dayton Journal Herald, (then the morning newspaper), I was assigned to cover the introduction of a local cookbook,* Keys to Our Kitchen, *produced by the Dayton Woman's Club. One of the first recipes I chose to make from the book was "Wonderful Cheesecake for*

8" on Page 229 contributed by a Mrs. L. Russell Wildasin. My father judged it the best cheesecake he had ever eaten. So did Grandma. She baked it for special occasions, including Rev. Puff's birthday.

Keys to Our Kitchen *is one of my prized cookbooks. It is out of print, but if you ever find one at a garage sale, be sure to buy it.*

"Grandma" and Mrs. Wildasin's Wonderful Cheesecake

Crust
1 ½ cups graham cracker crumbs
¼ cup sugar
Dash cinnamon
¼ cup butter, melted

Mix all the ingredients and place half the mixture in an eight-inch square baking pan or an eight-inch springform pan. Press firmly over bottom of pan and partially up the sides.

Filling
1 pound cream cheese
½ cup sugar
2 egg yolks
2 egg whites

With an electric mixer, mix cheese, sugar and egg yolks. In a separate bowl, beat whites until stiff. Fold whites into cheese mixture. Pour into crust in pan. Bake in a preheated 375-degree oven for 20 minutes. Cool 30 minutes.

Topping
2 cups sour cream
6 tablespoons sugar
2 teaspoons vanilla
Combine the topping ingredients and spread over

cake. Sprinkle reserved crumbs evenly over top of cake. Bake 10 to 12 minutes in a preheated 450-degree oven. Cool and refrigerate. Nine servings.

THE CRUST AND PUMPKIN SWIRLED THROUGH THE BATTER MAKE *for a delicious variation from a standard cheesecake. Beth Penza brought the cake to a fish fry we hosted in Worthington. Beth, who is married to Sam Penza, an oncologist at "The James" cancer hospital in Columbus, shares my addiction to reading cookbooks. Don't just read her recipe though; give it a try. I've modified her recipe by using reduced-fat cream cheese and no-calorie sweetener. For a richer taste, you can use sugar and regular cream cheese. You can prepare this in a traditional graham cracker crust, but the cookie crust is a nice touch.*

Beth's Pumpkin Swirl Cheesecake

Crust
2¼ cups gingersnap crumbs
½ cup pecans, finely chopped
⅓ cup butter or margarine, melted

Mix crumbs, nuts and butter. Press onto bottom and sides of an eight-inch springform pan or an eight-inch square baking pan. Bake 10 minutes in a preheated 350-degree oven.

Filling
3 packages (8 ounces each) reduced-fat
  cream cheese
1 cup no-calorie sweetener, such as Splenda,
  divided
1 teaspoon vanilla
3 eggs
1 cup canned pumpkin
1 teaspoon cinnamon

$\frac{1}{4}$ teaspoon nutmeg
Dash ground cloves

Beat cream cheese, $\frac{3}{4}$ cup sweetener and vanilla with electric mixer until blended. Add eggs, mixing at low speed, until blended. Reserve $1\frac{1}{2}$ cups batter. Add remaining $\frac{1}{4}$ cup sweetener, pumpkin and spices to remaining batter. Mix well. Spread half the pumpkin batter over the crust, then half the cream cheese batter. Repeat. Then cut through the batters with a knife several times to create a swirl effect.

In a preheated 350-degree oven, bake 55 to 60 minutes, or until center is almost set. Remove from the oven and, if using a springform pan, run a knife around the rim of the pan, but do not remove rim until cake is cool. Refrigerate four hours or overnight. If you use a square pan, do not remove cake; serve from the pan after chilling. Eight to 10 servings.

GRANDMA'S SPLATTERED RECIPE CARD SPECIFIED HER PREFERENCE *for Dutch cocoa for these moist cupcakes. She frosted them with only a thick curlicue of vanilla icing.*

Grandma's Never-Fail Chocolate Cupcakes

$\frac{1}{2}$ cup shortening, such as Crisco
$\frac{1}{2}$ cup Dutch cocoa, such as Droste's
$1\frac{1}{2}$ cups flour
$\frac{1}{2}$ cup buttermilk
1 cup sugar
1 teaspoon baking soda

1 teaspoon vanilla
1 egg
½ cup hot tap water

Put all ingredients into a bowl and beat well. Fill greased cupcake pans about ⅔ full. Bake in a preheated 325-degre oven 18 to 20 minutes, until a pick comes out clean. Makes about 12 standard-sized cupcakes. Frost as you like.

MILLIE BINGHAM — ALIAS KATE MACQUEEN, WRITER OF THE *syndicated Common Cents column — was Dayton's most famous bargain hunter. As her editor in the Lifestyle section of Dayton Daily News, I generally was bent over the computer when she went on shopping excursions. One day she instructed me to leave the office immediately to buy a beautifully styled black blazer that she had found for me. She insisted that it was such an incredible bargain that I couldn't pass it up. She had asked the clerk at Rike's Department Store to hold it for me. I dutifully left and came back triumphantly carrying my package. I still own that jacket more than 25 years later.*

Millie served this cake when the Lifestyle staff piled into her home for a potluck dinner.

Inimitable Millie's Chocolate Fudge Cake

Cake
2 cups flour
2 cups sugar (do not substitute a no-calorie
    sweetener)
1 stick margarine
3½ tablespoons cocoa
½ cup shortening, such as Crisco
1 cup water
½ cup buttermilk

1 teaspoon baking soda
1 teaspoon vanilla
2 eggs, slightly beaten

Mix flour and sugar in a large bowl. Put margarine, cocoa, shortening and water into a small saucepan and stir over medium heat. Bring to a slight bubbling state, stirring constantly. Add chocolate mixture to flour and sugar mixture. Stir well.

By hand or on slow speed of electric mixer, blend buttermilk, soda, vanilla and eggs into chocolate mixture. Pour into greased baking sheet. Important: use a large one, about 11x17 inches, with sides. Bake in a preheated 400-degree oven for 20 minutes. Meanwhile prepare the Fudge Topping.

Fudge Topping
1 stick margarine
3½ tablespoons cocoa
⅓ cup milk
1 teaspoon vanilla
1 pound confectioner's sugar

Put margarine, cocoa, milk and vanilla into a medium saucepan. Bring to a low boil, stirring constantly. Remove from heat. Add confectioner's sugar. Mix well. Spread over cake immediately after taking it out of the oven. Serve with vanilla ice cream. Twelve to 16 servings.

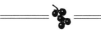

MOTHER PASSED THIS RECIPE ON TO ME AND I'VE MADE IT MORE *than any other. This is a super-moist cake. It's quick to make if you use ready-to-eat small carrots and use a food processor to shred them.*

Mother's Carrot Cake

2 cups sugar
2 cups flour
2 teaspoons baking soda
2 teaspoons cinnamon
1 ½ teaspoons salt
3 cups shredded carrots (about 1 pound)
1 ½ cups canola or other vegetable oil
4 eggs

Combine sugar, flour, baking soda, cinnamon and salt in a large bowl. Add and mix carrots, oil and eggs. Pour into an ungreased 9x13-inch baking pan. Bake in a 350-degree preheated oven 35 minutes, or until a pick comes out clean. Cool before frosting.

Cream Cheese Frosting
1 pound confectioner's sugar
8 ounces cream cheese
2 ounces margarine
1 teaspoon vanilla
Milk to thin, if necessary
¾ cup walnuts, chopped

With an electric mixer, combine sugar, cream cheese, margarine and vanilla. Add about a tablespoon of milk, if necessary, to make smooth and spreadable. Spread over cool cake. Garnish with chopped nuts. Twelve to 16 servings.

WHEN JIM AND I PURCHASED A HOME IN GEORGIA, THE FIRST *friends we contacted were Ron and Peg Trowbridge who were living in Middletown, Ohio, and scouring the country for an appropriate retirement location. Both were golfers, and like us,*

wanted a friendly climate. They checked out Reynolds Plantation and signed a contract on their first visit. They are good friends and golfing companions and Peg is an outstanding cook. This is her favorite cake and now one of ours as well.

Peg's Pumpkin Cake

4 eggs
1 cup vegetable oil, such as Wesson Oil
2 cups sugar
2 cups flour
2 teaspoons soda
2 teaspoons baking powder
2 teaspoons cinnamon
$\frac{1}{2}$ teaspoon salt
1 cup pumpkin

Mix the eggs, oil and sugar in a large bowl. Add flour, soda, baking powder, cinnamon and salt and beat. Add pumpkin and beat all ingredients together. Pour into two eight-or nine-inch greased pans and bake in a preheated 350-degree oven for 35 to 40 minutes, until a toothpick comes out clean. Cool and frost.

Frosting

1 stick margarine at room temperature
8 ounces cream cheese at room temperature
1 pound confectioner's sugar
$\frac{1}{2}$ teaspoon vanilla
1 cup pecans, chopped

Blend all ingredients together with an electric mixer and spread on cooled cake layers. Ten to 12 servings.

JIM AND I WERE STUNNED TO HEAR THE VOICE MAIL MESSAGE FROM *a good friend, saying that St. Elizabeth Medical Center had closed. It was ironic that at the time we got the word, we were vacationing in Alaska with Skip (Dr. Blaine Block) and his wife Janie. So far away from home, we mourned our loss together. Both Jim and Skip had been on the medical staff of St. E's for years; I had been the head of marketing. We held the organization in great esteem. At first we could not speak. Then the feelings tumbled out of us as we relived our years of working there with a staff of truly caring people, from nursing personnel to administrative support staff to cafeteria and maintenance workers. I had never worked anywhere where there were such loyal employees with such a strong sense of commitment to purpose.*

Barbara Bolser, the marketing department's secretary, came to my mind first. She carried out her responsibilities with goodness and grace. What's more, she always kindly noted my birthday by baking a cake.

The first time she served this cake at the office, she was secretive about the key ingredient until everyone on the staff raved about the taste. Then she confessed that it was prunes – that fruit that traditionally has gotten so little respect. Now, you'll notice, the packages are marked 'dried plums' so there's no need to be coy about the cake's content. This recipe was passed on to Barb by another dedicated secretary at St. E, Jan Wiltshire. It is best to make this moist cake a day or two before you plan to serve it.

Barb's Secret-Ingredient Birthday Cake

1 cup vegetable oil
1 ½ cups sugar
3 eggs
2 cups flour
1 teaspoon salt
1 teaspoon baking soda
1 teaspoon cinnamon
1 teaspoon allspice
1 teaspoon nutmeg

1 teaspoon vanilla
1 cup cooked, chopped, pitted dried plums (prunes)
1 cup walnuts, chopped
1 cup buttermilk

Mix all ingredients in a large bowl. Pour into a lightly greased 9x13-inch baking pan. Bake about 40 minutes or until pick comes out clean *at 350°*

Topping   (Prepare while cake is baking)

1 cup sugar
½ cup buttermilk
¼ pound butter or margarine
2 tablespoons light corn syrup
½ teaspoon baking soda

Place all ingredients into a large saucepan and heat until boiling. (Use a large pan because the soda makes it boil up high.) Cook about five minutes. It won't thicken.

Poke holes in the warm cake with a long wooden pick or skewer and pour warm topping over cake while still in the pan. Refrigerate overnight. Twelve to 16 servings.

IN 2003, THREE YEARS AFTER HIS RETIREMENT AS A PHYSICIAN AND *our relocation to Georgia, Jim returned to his profession. We were hesitant to give up our freedom, but Holzer Clinic and Holzer Medical Center in Gallipolis, Ohio, needed an oncologist on a temporary basis. Jim agreed to provide patient care for eight weeks. We gathered some belongings, particularly warmer clothing, and headed north for a short stint.*

As weeks went by, both of us grew fond of the people we met in the rural communities along the Ohio River, and we grew respectful of the care provided in the Holzer facilities. Evenings, Jim would tell me stories about the patients, other physicians and employees. The nurse assigned to work with Jim was Vicky Wilcox, a veteran Holzer nurse. He sang her praises; she was competent and caring and pleasant to work with. Looking back, I wondered if she had also been assigned to help recruit him. At any rate, he was recruited to be medical director of the new Holzer Center For Cancer Care, and we ended up staying almost three years.

Vicky treasures this old recipe from a faded 1934 newspaper clipping. Her grandmother, Mildred Hayes Miller, made this fruit cake that Vicky describes as "Oh, so good." She added that her grandmother wrapped the baked cakes in rum-soaked cheesecloth and stored them in a cool place for two weeks before serving them. I have not yet prepared this cake; if you try it, let me know how you like it. The original recipe mentioned salt in the directions, but did not indicate how much to add. I have guessed at one-half teaspoon. You might want to alter that.

This is another old recipe, like my grandma's mincemeat, that points out the patience of cooks long ago. We of the drive-through dinner generation want instant gratification, but folks in our grandmas' lifetimes waited a while for something good.

Vicky's Grandma's Fruit Cake

1 pound seeded raisins
½ pound dried currants or another ½ pound
   raisins
1 pound pitted dates
½ pound glace (candied) pineapple
½ pound glace (candied) cherries
1 pound nutmeats (walnuts or pecans)
¼ pound sliced citron
¼ pound sliced orange peel
¼ pound sliced lemon peel
3 cups all-purpose flour
½ teaspoon salt
1½ teaspoons cinnamon

1 teaspoon nutmeg
1 teaspoon allspice
½ teaspoon soda
½ pound butter or other fat
1 square chocolate, melted
½ cup grape juice
½ cup honey
1 cup sugar
6 eggs, beaten

Wash and drain currants thoroughly. Other packaged dried fruits do not require washings. Cut the dates in quarters, the pineapple into ½-inch wedges, and the cherries in halves. Cut or break the nuts into pieces; do not chop them. The citron, lemon and orange peel come already sliced. Mix the fruit and nuts together.

Sift the flour, salt, spices and soda over the fruit and nuts; mix with the finger tips until each piece is coated with flour. Cream the fat; stir in sugar gradually; then added beaten eggs and melted chocolate. Stir in floured fruits and nuts alternately with grape juice and honey. Pour into two round two-quart casseroles and one loaf pan. Bake at 225 degrees about three hours. (You might substitute three or four loaf pans for the two casseroles. If you do, test the loaf pans for doneness at about two and one-half hours.)

If you wish, soak strips of cheesecloth in rum and wrap the cooled loaves. Then wrap in foil and seal in an airtight container, such as a large plastic bag. Store in a cool spot for two weeks. Yields three to five loaves, depending on sizes of pans.

IN TERMS OF TEXTURE AND FLAVOR, THIS CAKE RANKS UP THERE WITH *carrot and pumpkin cakes. Hoping they had never sampled it before, I served this to Bob and Nancy Westfall when they were houseguests. It turns out this is the birthday cake that Nancy traditionally makes for one of her grandchildren. The child has good taste. This version is an adaptation of a cake included in the* Blue Willow Inn Cookbook. *If you are heading south, the Blue Willow Inn is a must stop. Located in Social Circle, Georgia, the restaurant is touted for its huge Southern buffet.*

It's-the-Berries Birthday Cake

Cake
1 package white or yellow cake mix
1 package (3 ounces) strawberry gelatin
    (sugar-free or regular)
⅔ cup vegetable oil
4 eggs
½ cup water
1 cup sliced strawberries, drained
    (fresh or frozen)
Cooking spray, such as Pam
1 tablespoon sugar

Combine the cake mix and gelatin in a large bowl. Add oil and then eggs. Mix thoroughly with an electric mixer at slow speed. Add water and strawberries and mix until they are well distributed in the batter. Spray angel food cake pan or Bundt cake pan with cooking spray and sprinkle bottom and sides with sugar. In preheated 350-degree oven, bake 40-45 minutes or until pick comes out clean. Cool thoroughly on a wire rack before removing cake from pan, but do not turn pan upside down while cooling. (I made that mistake once!)

Frosting
1 pound confectioner's sugar

¼ pound butter, softened
1 teaspoon vanilla
¼ cup sliced fresh strawberries
Milk, if needed
Extra strawberries for garnish (optional)

Combine confectioner's sugar, butter, vanilla and strawberries in a medium bowl and mix with an electric beater until smooth. Add small amount of milk, if necessary to achieve spreading consistency. Optional: garnish with fresh strawberry halves. About 12 servings.

A NEW COUPLE MOVED IN NEXT TO OUR GEORGIA HOME WHILE WE *were living temporarily in West Virginia. We didn't know what to expect when we returned, but we soon discovered we couldn't have better neighbors if we hand-picked them.*

Originally from Long Island, Susan and Bruce Punger host dinner parties that are punctuated by lots of laughter. Bruce, a retired New York City harbor pilot, regales us with descriptions of his career's perils and pleasures, and master story-teller Susan offers unbelievable memories of growing up in a family of 14.

This is one of Susan's delicious desserts.

Susan's Chocolate Chip Cake

1 box butter recipe cake mix, such as
    Duncan Hines
1 small box vanilla instant pudding mix
1 bag (12 ounces) semi-sweet chocolate chips
4 eggs
1 cup milk
1 cup vegetable oil, such as canola

In a food processor or a blender, grind half the

chocolate chips until they are close to a powdery consistency. Save the other half of the chips for later.

Place the powdered chips in a large bowl with the cake mix, pudding mix, eggs, milk and oil. Blend with an electric mixer until it is a smooth batter. Place mixture in a greased, lightly floured Bundt pan.

Sprinkle remaining chips on top and immediately place in a preheated 350-degree oven for about an hour, until a pick comes out clean. Cool completely. Remove from pan and sprinkle with confectioner's sugar. About 12 servings.

JENNI AND GREG'S PATERNAL GREAT-GRANDMOTHER, JENNIE *Marshall, lived in one of the oldest stone houses in Muskingum County, Ohio, when I first met her. She was a frail lady who sat serenely in her rocker when we visited. But she always found the energy to bake a batch of these tender cookies before our arrival. The texture distinguishes them.*

Grandma Marshall's Iced Pineapple Cookies

1 cup light brown sugar
1 cup granulated sugar
1 cup margarine
2 eggs
1 20-ounce can crushed pineapple, drained (reserve the juice)
1 teaspoon vanilla
1 teaspoon baking soda
1 teaspoon baking powder
¼ teaspoon salt
3½ cups flour

In a large bowl, cream the sugars and margarine with an electric mixer. At low speed, mix in the eggs, pineapple, vanilla, baking soda, baking powder, salt and flour. The batter should be slightly stiff. Drop the batter by tablespoon on a greased cookie sheet about 1 ½ inches apart. Bake 10 to 12 minutes in 375-degree preheated oven. Cool on a wire rack. Makes three dozen cookies.

Icing

2 cups confectioner's sugar
¼ cup butter at room temperature
3 to 4 tablespoons reserved pineapple juice

Cream sugar and butter. Mix in juice to spreading consistency. Frost cookies when they are cool. (If you prefer a glazed look, frost while warm.)

M Y GRANDMOTHER HAD AMAZINGLY LOW CHOLESTEROL LEVELS. *I sometimes wonder if this phenomenon was related to the amount of oatmeal cookies she baked and ate. To keep the cookies soft, she stored them in an airtight container with a slice of fresh bread laid on top of them.*

Grandma's Soft Oatmeal Cookies

1 cup shortening, such as Crisco
1 cup granulated sugar
1 cup light brown sugar
3 eggs
2 tablespoons water
1 ½ teaspoons vanilla
2 cups flour, sifted
1 teaspoon salt
1 teaspoon baking powder

1 teaspoon baking soda
3 teaspoons cinnamon
$\frac{1}{2}$ teaspoon nutmeg
$2\frac{1}{2}$ cups old-fashioned oatmeal (not quick oats)
1 cup raisins
1 cup walnuts, chopped

In a large bowl, cream the shortening and sugars. Add eggs, water and vanilla and mix thoroughly. Add flour, salt, baking powder and soda, spices and oats. Stir. Mix in raisins and nuts. Drop by tablespoon onto greased cookie sheet. Bake in 350-degree preheated oven 12 to 15 minutes. Makes about three dozen cookies.

THESE WEDDING COOKIES WERE STANDARDS IN GRANDMA'S *Christmas baking routine, along with Taffy Tarts and Lemon Squares. She made hundreds of the cookies and delivered them to us in coat-sized gift boxes layered with waxed paper.*

Grandma's Mexican Wedding Cookies

1 cup margarine, softened
$\frac{1}{2}$ cup confectioner's sugar
$2\frac{1}{2}$ cups flour
$\frac{1}{4}$ teaspoon salt
$\frac{1}{4}$ cup walnuts, ground fine
1 teaspoon vanilla
Additional confectioner's sugar, about 2 cups

Using an electric mixer, cream margarine and sugar and add flour, salt, nuts and vanilla. Mix until batter sticks together. Mix in additional flour, if necessary, to get batter to stick together. Roll into walnut-sized balls and place on lightly greased baking sheet. Flatten slightly with back of spoon. Bake 20 minutes in a 350-degree preheated oven. Immediately roll in confectioner's sugar. Cool and roll again in confectioner's sugar. Makes about 2½ dozen cookies.

TIM GAFFNEY IS ONE OF THE BEST WRITERS I EVER HIRED. A VETERAN Dayton Daily News *reporter, he has authored several books. My favorite is "Grandpa Takes Me to the Moon." Tim also makes good cookies. He brought these to a staff party one night and I requested the recipe. Grandma borrowed it and adopted these cookies as one of her holiday offerings.*

Tim and Grandma's Lemon Squares

½ pound butter, softened (don't be tempted
  to use margarine)
½ cup confectioner's sugar
2⅓ cups flour, divided
4 eggs, slightly beaten
2 cups sugar
½ cup lemon juice, squeezed fresh or bottled
1 teaspoon baking powder
3 tablespoons confectioner's sugar

Lightly grease a 9x13-inch cake pan. In a large bowl, cream butter and ½ cup confectioner's sugar. Add two cups of the flour and mix well. Press mixture into bottom of pan. Bake 20 minutes in a 350-degree preheated oven. Meanwhile, beat eggs with sugar, lemon juice, baking powder and the remaining ⅓ cup flour. Pour mixture over warm, baked crust and bake an additional 25 to 30 minutes, until lightly browned and set. Cool and sprinkle evenly with confectioner's sugar. Cut into 24 squares.

YOU NEED MINI-MUFFIN PANS TO MAKE THESE PASTRIES, WHICH *resemble miniature pecan pies. Make the pastry the day before baking the cookies.*

Grandma's Taffy Tarts

Pastry
1 cup margarine, softened
1 package (8 ounces) cream cheese, softened
(reduced-fat is fine)
2⅓ cups flour

With an electric mixer, blend margarine and cheese. Add flour. Work into a smooth ball, wrap in waxed paper and chill overnight.

Filling
2 eggs
1½ cups dark brown sugar
2 tablespoons melted margarine
2 teaspoons vanilla
2 cups pecans, chopped

In a medium-sized bowl, beat eggs slightly; stir in brown sugar and margarine. Add vanilla and nuts. Stir.

Break off walnut-sized pieces of pastry and roll into balls. (For easy handling, work with one-half the pastry at a time; keep rest in refrigerator.) Press the pastry balls into mini-muffin pans, forming cups for the filling. Spoon filling into each. Bake in 350-degree preheated oven about 22 minutes. Do not overbake or filling will dry out. Remove from pans and cool on wire rack. Makes about 3½ dozen cookies.

MOTHER BOILED A METAL THIMBLE TO STERILIZE IT BEFORE WE *made these cookies. If you don't have a thimble, use a clean thumb. For the holidays, use mint jelly in some and strawberry jam in others.*

Mother's Thimble Cookies

1 cup flour
Dash salt
$\frac{1}{2}$ cup butter or margarine
3 tablespoons confectioner's sugar
1 cup finely chopped pecans
1 teaspoon vanilla
Jam or jelly

Sift flour and salt onto waxed paper or into a bowl. In a medium-sized bowl, cream butter or margarine with confectioner's sugar. Stir in the flour-salt mixture. Blend well to make a soft dough. Stir in nuts and vanilla. Chill in the refrigerator several hours or overnight.

Shape the dough into walnut-sized balls. Place two inches apart on a greased cookie sheet. Make an indentation in the center of each ball with a thimble or your thumb. Fill with about $\frac{1}{4}$ teaspoon jelly. Bake in 300-degree preheated oven for 22 minutes or until slightly browned. Remove from cookie sheets and cool on wire rack. Makes about $2\frac{1}{2}$ dozen cookies.

THESE ARE SOFT COOKIES SIMILAR TO THE BIG ONES YOU CAN BUY *at the bakery. They are drop cookies — no cookie cutter is used.*

Mother's Soft Sugar Cookies

4 cups flour
1 teaspoon baking soda
1 teaspoon salt
1 cup shortening, such as Crisco
2 cups sugar
2 eggs, separated
1 cup buttermilk
1 generous teaspoon vanilla
Sugar sprinkles (optional)
Frosting (optional)

In a large bowl, mix the flour, soda and salt and blend in the shortening and sugar. In a separate medium-sized bowl, mix two egg yolks with the buttermilk and vanilla. Combine the egg mixture with the flour mixture. Then fold in two egg whites that have been beaten stiff.

Drop by heaping teaspoon onto greased cookie sheet. Bake 10 to 12 minutes in a 375-degree preheated oven. Add baking time if you make larger cookies. Frost with your favorite icing and top with sprinkles, if you like. Makes about four dozen small cookies.

SON-IN-LAW NED'S MOTHER, KRISTINA SORMAZ, EMIGRATED FROM *Europe as a young woman. Austrian born, she married a native of Bosnia, and as a result has a diverse stockpile of old-country recipes. She prepares this cookie each year for Ned's "slava" – a feast that commemorates his "name day," the day of the birth of the saint for which he was named. It is like a Thanksgiving celebration that focuses on glorifying God and paying honor to the unifying force of family.*

Kris's Russian Pita Cookies

Crust
3 sticks butter at room temperature
3 ½ cups flour
1 ⅓ cups confectioner's sugar
1 egg
Additional flour for board

Blend butter and flour together with a pastry cutter. Add egg and confectioner's sugar and mix. Form dough into a ball and divide into two parts. On a floured board, roll each part into a 9x13-inch rectangle.

Filling
6 eggs
3 cups confectioner's sugar
3 tablespoons breadcrumbs
3 cups ground walnuts

Separate yolks from whites. In a large bowl, beat egg whites until stiff. In a medium-sized bowl, mix egg yolks and sugar together. Then fold egg yolk mixture, breadcrumbs and walnuts into the stiff egg whites.

Lay one rectangle of dough into a greased and floured 9x13-inch baking pan. Spread filling on crust. Place remaining layer of dough on top.

Bake in a 300-degree preheated oven for one hour. Cool and cut into bars, squares or diamond shapes. Makes about 24 cookies.

D AYTON FRIENDS, BELLA AND MIKE FREEMAN, ARE HOUSEGUESTS *who arrive with warm greetings and armloads of food. Dietician Bella brought these chocolate treats when they visited our Lake Erie cottage. If you are a chocoholic, this is for you.*

Bella's Double-Frosted Brownies

Brownie

2 ounces unsweetened chocolate
$\frac{1}{4}$ pound margarine
1 cup sugar
2 eggs
$\frac{2}{3}$ cup flour
$\frac{1}{2}$ teaspoon baking powder
$\frac{1}{4}$ teaspoon salt
1 teaspoon vanilla
6 ounces chocolate chips

Melt chocolate and margarine together. Add sugar and eggs and beat. Mix in flour, baking powder, salt, vanilla and chocolate chips. Put in a greased 8x8-inch baking pan and bake in 350-degree preheated oven for 25 minutes. Turn off heat and leave in oven five more minutes.

First Frosting

1 cup confectioner's sugar
2 tablespoons butter, softened
1 tablespoon milk
$\frac{1}{2}$ tablespoon flavoring (vanilla, mint or liqueur
    of your choice)

Beat sugar, butter, milk and flavoring and spread on cooled brownies.

Second Frosting

2 ounces semi-sweet or bittersweet chocolate

1 tablespoon butter

Melt chocolate and butter in a small saucepan and spread on first frosting. Cool. Cut into 12 squares.

I N THE MIDST OF SORROW, WE FIND COMFORT IN FRIENDS, FAMILY *and good food as well. The weeks preceding our friend Skip Block's death, his children and their spouses cooked in his kitchen. Skip was unable to enjoy these meals, but they brought us together as a family — even those of us who were unrelated. These rich cookies were the specialty of his daughter, Cathy Block Hirschhorn.*

Cathy's Fudge Squares

Cake
2 sticks butter
3 heaping tablespoons cocoa
1 teaspoon vanilla
1 cup sugar
3 eggs, well beaten
½ cup flour

Melt the butter and add remaining ingredients. Beat well with an electric mixer. Pour into a lightly greased 8-inch square baking pan. Bake in a 350-degree preheated oven for 25 to 30 minutes, until a pick comes out clean.

Icing (prepare this while cake is baking)
½ stick butter
2 tablespoons cocoa
1 teaspoon vanilla
2½ cups confectioner's sugar
2 to 3 tablespoons milk

Melt butter. Add remaining ingredients and beat together with an electric mixer. Frost the cake immediately after removing it from the oven. Cut into 16 squares.

T HE TEXTURE OF THESE CHOCOLATE BARS THAT DAUGHTER-IN-LAW *Carrie bakes differentiates them from other chocolate cookies. She used vanilla wafer crumbs. I substituted chocolate graham cracker crumbs: the more chocolate, the better. Ignore the calories and enjoy.*

Carrie's Chocolate Bars

1 ½ cups chocolate graham cracker crumbs
¼ cup margarine or butter, melted
¾ cup heavy whipping cream
1 cup semi-sweet chocolate chips
3 eggs
⅔ cup sugar
⅛ teaspoon salt
Chocolate topping

Crust
Mix crumbs and melted butter. Press into an ungreased 8 or 9-inch square baking pan. Bake in a 350-degree preheated oven for 10 minutes.

Cake
Heat whipping cream and chocolate chips over low heat, stirring frequently until chocolate melts. Remove from heat. Cool five minutes. Beat eggs, sugar and salt in a large bowl until foamy. Pour chocolate mixture into egg mixture and stir. Pour over baked crust.

Bake at 350 degrees 25 to 35 minutes or until center springs back when lightly touched. Cool 15 minutes.

Topping
$\frac{1}{2}$ cup semi-sweet chocolate chips
1 tablespoon shortening, such as Crisco

Heat chips and shortening in a small pan over low heat, stirring frequently until melted. Spread topping on baked cake. Refrigerate until chilled, about two hours. Cut into 16 squares or bars.

FLORENCE AND TOM DENNISON WELCOMED US TO OUR NEW GEORGIA *home with a homemade cookie mix arranged in a dressed-up canning jar. The brownie mix makes a good hostess gift as well.*

Florence's Brownies in a Jar

1 cup flour
$\frac{1}{2}$ teaspoon salt

Mix flour and salt together. Spoon the mixture evenly into a one-quart canning jar with a lid.

In a similar manner, add the following ingredients, one layer at a time, tapping after each to settle the ingredients.

6 tablespoons unsweetened cocoa
$\frac{3}{4}$ cup granulated sugar
$\frac{1}{2}$ cup (packed) light brown sugar
$\frac{3}{4}$ cup granulated sugar
6 tablespoons unsweetened cocoa
$\frac{1}{2}$ cup walnuts, chopped

$\frac{1}{4}$ cup white chocolate chips
$\frac{1}{4}$ cup semisweet chocolate chips

Close the lid. (If you wish, decorate the lid with gingham or other fabric and tie with a ribbon.) Type the following baking instructions on a colorful paper or cardstock and tie to the jar.

Brownies in a Jar
To bake: Heat oven to 350 degrees. Grease a 9-inch square pan. Put brownie mix in a bowl and stir. Add $\frac{1}{2}$ cup melted butter, 3 beaten eggs and $\frac{1}{2}$ teaspoon vanilla. Stir well. Spread into pan. Bake about 35 minutes, until toothpick inserted in center has a few crumbs. Cool and enjoy.

AS FAR AS I CAN TELL, THERE IS NO ITALIAN HERITAGE IN OUR *family; we have Germanic background plus some English in us. So I don't know how Aunt Thelma became enamored with making Italian pizzelles. She made hundreds of them at Christmas time, wrapping them in plastic, tying on a ribbon and presenting them as gifts.*

It is a tradition that she, in her mid eighties, has only recently given up; it takes hours of her time, as her daughter Nancy Smith, will tell you. When Nancy e-mailed Aunt T's recipe, she enclosed this note: "Let me warn you, these cookies take forever to make. I made two and gave up. Happy baking!"

You will need a pizzelle maker. My electric model comes with inserts for making not only pizzelles, but Belgian waffles and grilled sandwiches as well.

Aunt Thelma's Italian Pizzelles

3 eggs beaten
$\frac{3}{4}$ cup sugar
$\frac{3}{4}$ cup butter or margarine, melted

1 ½ to 2 cups flour
1 teaspoon baking powder
2 teaspoons vanilla
1 teaspoon anise seed or extract
Butter or shortening for greasing grill
Confectioner's sugar (about ½ cup)

Place all ingredients, except confectioner's sugar, in a large bowl and beat with an electric mixer. If you use the smaller amount of flour, the pizzelles will be thin; they will be thicker if you add more flour. Preheat pizzelle iron; then lightly grease it. Drop about a tablespoon of batter onto the center of the iron. It will take some practice to get just the right amount. Close the lid tight. If the batter oozes out, cut off the edges immediately. Bake about 30 seconds, until steaming stops. The cookies should be golden. Remove with fork. Cool on wire rack or clean tea towels. Dust with confectioner's sugar. Makes about two dozen cookies.

Variations

Lemon pizzelle: Omit vanilla and anise. Replace with two teaspoons lemon extract and one tablespoon grated lemon peel.

Chocolate pizzelle: To basic recipe, add three tablespoons cocoa and three tablespoons sugar.

Nut pizzelle: To basic recipe, add 1 ½ cups ground nuts.

MY AUNT THELMA NEWPORT KUBILIUS IS THE ONLY SURVIVING *offspring of my maternal grandparents, Stella and Homer Newport. One baby died in infancy. Mother — Dorotha — was the eldest child. My Uncle Denver (Denny) and Aunt Thelma were in the middle, and my Aunt Zelpha was the baby.*

MOTHER (DOROTHA) AT LEFT, AND SISTERS THELMA AND ZELPHA WERE NAMED FOR THEIR MIDWIVES

Did you catch those sisters' names? Dorotha, Thelma, Zelpha. The three—believe it or not – were named for the midwives who delivered them. I don't know how Uncle Denny got his name.

In fact, I know little about the Newport family history, but my cousin Paul, Zelpha's firstborn, knows a great deal. A genealogy hobbyist, he has identified our German and English heritage.

After their marriage, Aunt Zelpha and her husband Edward Bastian moved to Marion, Ohio, where cousin Paul and his brother David grew up. We saw them infrequently. Paul recalls that his paternal Grandmother Bastian taught his mother about cooking.

This is one of the cookies passed down through the Bastian family. Paul slices them thin when he bakes them. They will be crisp and are good with tea. I tried slicing them thick and they resulted in a soft cookie, best eaten warm. If you want to rewarm them, simply nuke them a few seconds and their softness is restored.

Bastian Family's Butterscotch Cookie

2 cups dark brown sugar
½ cup butter, softened

About 3 cups flour
1 teaspoon cream of tartar
1 teaspoon baking soda
2 eggs

Cream the sugar and butter together. Mix in the cream of tartar, soda, eggs and enough flour to make a stiff dough. Shape into two long rolls, wrap in waxed paper and place in refrigerator overnight.

Cut in $\frac{1}{4}$-inch or up to $\frac{3}{4}$-inch slices and place on a lightly greased cookie sheet. Bake seven to nine minutes, depending on how thick you sliced the cookies, in a preheated 400-degree oven. Watch closely; the cookies burn easily. Yields three to four dozen cookies, depending on how thick you slice them.

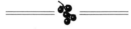

FRIEND ANITA RICHWINE PRIZES HER ITALIAN HERITAGE AND THIS *family recipe. Biscotti are twice-baked crunchy cookies. Italians dip them in wine, but they are good dipped in tea too.*

Anita's Mother's Biscotti

1 cup sugar
1 cup shortening, such as Crisco
4 eggs
4 cups flour
4 teaspoons baking powder
1 teaspoon vanilla
Scant $\frac{1}{2}$ cup milk

Using a mixer, cream sugar and shortening. Add four eggs, one at a time, beating after each addition. In another bowl, mix by hand the flour and baking powder. Alternately, add sugar-shortening-egg mix and the vanilla and milk to the flour mixture. Dough will be soft. Divide dough into four equal parts. Shape each part into a long, narrow loaf about 1 ½ to 2 inches wide. Place loaves on a large, greased cookie sheet. Bake in a preheated 400-degree oven for 18 minutes. Remove from oven, cool slightly and then cut diagonally into ¾-inch slices. Place slices close together on an ungreased cookie sheet and bake at 350 degrees about 12 minutes, or until golden brown. Makes about 3 ½ dozen cookies.

THESE COOKIES ARE SIMPLE TO MAKE, AND ONCE YOU BAKE THEM, *I guarantee you will make them over and over. One Christmas, Nancy Hines gave us a batch in a shiny red canister. I'm told they keep well in an airtight container, but ours never last long enough to prove that theory.*

Nancy's Graham Cracker Pralines

12 graham cracker sheets
½ cup pecans, chopped
2 sticks butter
1 cup dark brown sugar

Divide each graham cracker into four pieces, breaking on the perforations. Place in a single layer on a 15x10-inch baking sheet with a rim. Sprinkle pecans on top.

In a saucepan, melt butter and sugar. Bring to a boil and boil one minute. The mixture will thicken slightly. Remove from heat and spoon evenly over the crackers. Put into a preheated oven at 400 degrees for about three to four minutes. Watch carefully and remove from the oven when bubbles begin to form on top of the cookies. Transfer cookies from pan to a sheet of foil to cool. Keep in tins or freeze in plastic bags for up to three months. Makes 48 small cookies.

PENNY DARCY, MY FORMER SISTER-IN-LAW, AND I WERE THE "GALLEY *girls"* *as we and our husbands Jim and Jack cruised out of Seattle aboard a chartered boat. We had the boat heavily provisioned for many meals aboard. As we approached Canadian waters, the captain asked if we had any cigarettes aboard or any fruit with pits. We did not have cigarettes, but we had pounds of gorgeous ripening peaches. He told us to throw them overboard because we couldn't take anything with pits inside the Canadian borders. We were miffed. We promptly pared those peaches and ditched the pits in the deep briny on the American side.*

Soon a Canadian authority boarded the boat and asked the anticipated questions; "Do you have weapons aboard?" No. "Do you have cigarettes?" No. "What about alcohol?" Just the amount permitted. He asked other questions, and we smugly awaited the question about pits. He never asked.

Well, needless to say, we had a lot of peaches to eat fast. We made a juicy cobbler that was so good that we baked it on every subsequent cruise.

Penny's Peachy Cobbler

4 cups peeled and sliced firm-ripe peaches
     (about 8 medium peaches)
½ cup sugar
2 teaspoons lemon juice
½ teaspoon cinnamon
2 cups fresh blueberries
1 ½ cups flour
½ cup sugar
¾ cup butter or margarine

½ teaspoon nutmeg
Vanilla ice cream

In a 9x12-inch baking dish, mix together peaches, sugar, lemon juice and cinnamon. Sprinkle blueberries over peaches.

In a food processor or with a pastry cutter or using your fingers, combine the flour, sugar, butter, and nutmeg until the mixture has the texture of coarse cornmeal. Squeeze topping to compact it; then crumble it over the fruit. Bake in preheated 375-degree oven about 45 minutes, until golden and bubbling. Serve warm, topped with ice cream. Eight servings.

NO DOUBT ABOUT IT: 7-UP WAS GRANDMA'S FAVORITE SOFT DRINK. *She drank it, put it into gelatin salads, made 7-Up floats and featured it in the sauce for these scrumptious dumplings. Use Fuji or Granny Smith apples when you prepare this dish. If the crusts brown too fast, cover lightly with foil the last 10 or 15 minutes of baking.*

Grandma's Apple Dumplings

Sauce
20 ounces 7-Up
1½ cups sugar
¼ teaspoon cinnamon
¼ teaspoon nutmeg

Combine 7-Up, sugar, cinnamon and nutmeg in a saucepan and stir over medium heat until sugar dissolves. Set aside.

Dumplings
6 medium-sized apples, peeled and cored

2 cups flour, sifted
1 teaspoon salt
2 teaspoons baking powder
¾ cup shortening, such as Crisco
½ cup milk
6 tablespoons sugar
1 teaspoon cinnamon
3 teaspoons butter
Additional butter, about 3 tablespoons

Combine flour, salt and baking powder. Add shortening and milk and mix well. Roll into six 7-inch squares. Place apple in the center of each square. Combine the sugar and cinnamon and place one tablespoon of the mixture in the center of each apple. Place ½ teaspoon butter on each. Fold up the corners of the pastry and pinch the edges together. Arrange dumplings in a greased 9x13x2-inch baking pan. Pour prepared sauce over them. Dot with additional butter. Bake in preheated 425-degree oven about 35 minutes. Serves ~~eight~~. *Six.*

"**S**HERBERT" – THAT'S HOW MY FAMILY MISSPELLED AND INCORRECTLY *pronounced the word. The correct spelling of this icy dessert is "sherbet." However you pronounce it, it's a perfect cooler on a steamy summer day. You do not need an ice cream maker to prepare this dessert.*

Grandma's Pineapple Sherbet

2 cups buttermilk
½ cup sugar
1 cup crushed pineapple, drained
1 egg white
1½ teaspoons vanilla

Mix buttermilk, sugar and pineapple. Place it in a plastic container and put it into the freezer. Freeze until mushy. Then put mixture into a chilled bowl. In a separate bowl, beat egg white (use a pasteurized egg to be safe) with vanilla and fold into mixture. Freeze several hours. Four servings.

FRESH OUT OF COLLEGE, ED MILLER, A MIDDLETOWN, OHIO, *native, began his healthcare career as an administrative aide at St. Elizabeth Medical Center in Dayton. He offered this show-piece dessert at an office gathering. The presentation is impressive and it tastes as good as it looks.*

Ed's Dessert Pizza

1 package (18 ounces) refrigerated sugar cookie
    dough
1 package (8 ounces) cream cheese
1/3 cup sugar
$\frac{1}{2}$ teaspoon vanilla
1 cup strawberries, sliced
2 kiwi fruit, pared and sliced thin
2 or 3 canned pineapple rings, cut into small wedges
$\frac{1}{2}$ cup grapes, sliced in half
(You can use any combination of fruit. Blueberries
    are good; mandarin oranges look pretty.)
$\frac{1}{2}$ cup orange marmalade, heated

Press cookie dough evenly into an ungreased pizza pan. Bake 12 to 15 minutes, or until pastry is slightly brown. Cool completely. *at 350°*

In a small bowl, combine cream cheese, sugar and vanilla and beat with electric mixer until smooth. Spread over cooled cookie crust. Arrange your choice of fruit over the cream cheese. Spoon the warm marmalade over the fruit. Refrigerate at least an hour before serving. Cut into wedges or squares. Refrigerate any remaining pizza. Serves eight to 12.

For 12 years Janice and Tom Vance operated a small Victorian bed and breakfast beside their home at the confluence of the Kanawha and Ohio Rivers in Point Pleasant, West Virginia. They welcomed people from various parts of the world to the charming house that they had painstakingly restored.

Late in 2003, when Jim began working at the Holzer Center for Cancer Care in Gallipolis, we approached the Vances to ask if we could occupy the bed and breakfast for two years. Jim was taken by the place at first sight. "It's exactly like my grandma's house," he said.

The Vances gave our question consideration and kindly allowed us to move in, with Janice commenting, "You don't need to bring a thing." We brought very little. We lived amid the Vances' antiques and collectibles and ate off their china and slept in their four-poster bed.

We could not have found a finer site or better neighbors. "Stone Manor," as the house was called, was built in 1885 by riverboat Captain J.H. Stone. It faces Tu-Endie-Wei Park, a popular tourist destination which is officially marked as the site of the first battle of the Revolutionary War. It is also the burial ground for Chief Cornstalk and Mad Anne Bailey. American history buffs will recognize these names. From our windows we could view both rivers and revel in the sight of the sun setting over the Ohio River.

One thing Janice did not provide was breakfast, but she frequently brought us treats. This recipe has passed through generations of Janice's family.

Janice's Bananas with Brown Sugar Dressing

1 cup light brown sugar
2 tablespoons flour

1 egg, slightly beaten
3 tablespoons vinegar
1 cup water
3 bananas, cut in half and then cut
    again lengthwise
½ cup salted peanuts, crushed

Mix brown sugar and flour in a small saucepan. Add small amounts of egg, vinegar and water to make a paste; then slowly add remaining egg, vinegar and water. Cook on medium heat until mixture thickens. Cool.

Top sliced bananas with cooled dressing and sprinkle nuts on top. Makes six servings of half a banana per person.

FOLKS STIR COCA COLA INTO THEIR CAKE BATTER IN GEORGIA, WHERE *the soft drink company is headquartered. But I never heard of root beer cake until Jim came home from the Holzer Center for Cancer Care with the recipe. Demmie Hanna brought the cake in to share with co-workers, and Jim blissfully indulged. Demmie's recipe calls for frosting the cake with whipped topping mixed with a little root beer, but the recipe below offers a glaze alternative.*

Demmie's Root Beer Cake

Cake
1 package white or yellow cake mix
1 ¼ cups root beer
2 eggs
¼ cup vegetable oil

Combine cake mix, root beer, eggs and oil and beat two minutes with an electric mixer on low speed. Beat one minute longer on high speed. Pour into a lightly greased 13x9-inch baking pan and bake in a preheated 350-degree oven for 35 to 40 minutes, until a pick inserted in the center comes out clean.

Glaze
¾ cup confectioner's sugar
5 tablespoons root beer

Beat confectioner's sugar with root beer until mixture is smooth. Thin with additional root beer, if necessary, to make a syrupy consistency. Poke holes in warm cake with toothpick. Pour glaze over warm cake. Serve with vanilla ice cream. Makes 12 to 16 servings.

TOM AND LYNNE ROACH WERE AMONG OUR FIRST FRIENDS *when we settled in Georgia. As realtors, they were patient and unflappable. We bought the house so impulsively that we forgot to ask questions about lot lines, type of heating, and all those important factors we tell our children to thoroughly investigate before making a major purchase. I called Tom many times after we signed on the dotted line to ask what he may have considered foolish questions.*

After our move, we shared many meals in our home and in theirs. Our hearts were heavy when Tom was diagnosed with cancer. We watched Lynne deal with the greatest of life's trials with strength, faith and grace. Tom's gone, but Lynne will never be alone. Her positive spirit prevails as she fills her home with family and friends. This is a dessert she served at a small dinner party. I've revised her Martha Stewart original to lower the calories a bit.

Lynne's Fruit Tart

Cooking spray, such as Pam

3 apples or pears
¾ cup fat-free milk
¼ cup butter, melted
⅓ cup sugar or no-calorie sweetener, such
    as Splenda
⅓ cup flour
2 teaspoons vanilla
3 eggs
¼ teaspoon salt
Confectioner's sugar
Strawberries or blueberries (optional)

Peel, halve and core the fruit. Slice the fruit lengthwise in ¼-inch slices. In a nine-inch pie pan greased with cooking spray, arrange slices in a slightly overlapping circular pattern; set aside.

In a blender, process melted butter, milk, sugar or sweetener, flour, vanilla, eggs and salt until smooth. Pour batter over fruit and bake 40 to 45 minutes in a 350-degree preheated oven, until slightly browned. Dust with confectioner's sugar and serve warm. Garnish with berries. Serves six.

Turtles in the Basement

I NEVER WITNESSED GREAT GRANDMA WEGHORN COMMIT THE *heinous deed, but by the time I was six years old, I knew the preliminaries well. Timidly I followed her as she bustled to the curb when the open-bed truck rattled up, its wooden crates teetering as the driver jerked to a stop in front of her red brick bungalow on Notre Dame Avenue in Old North Dayton.*

This part of the city was populated by German, Lithuanian, Hungarian and Polish immigrants. The chicken man had good customers in the neighborhood so he visited weekly.

A SERIOUS-LOOKING FAMILY: GREAT GRANDMA WEGHORN IS IN FRONT ROW; MY GRANDMA IS IN BACK

I peeked from behind Great Grandma's wide body as she authoritatively examined the fowl and selected two plump hens. She made quick payment and bundled the ill-fated creatures in her long apron. Amid frenzied squawking and feathers flying, she retreated to her house and dispatched me to my own just three doors away.

Crescentia Weghorn was a stern, German-born hausfrau who wore round eyeglasses, ankle-length dresses and sensible shoes. Although she was good to me, I don't recall seeing her smile. She looked particularly sinister when she headed for her kitchen with those chickens.

For a while, Mother occupied me at our house, but inevitably I wandered back up the street to play in Grandma's backyard. There, securely fastened on the clothesline, were the headless forms hanging upside down, the blood draining from their lifeless bodies.

M Y CHILDREN'S FAST-FOOD GENERATION HAS LITTLE COMPREHENSION *of the effort my great grandparents and grandparents expended to put dinner on the table. In the 1940s and 1950s, families planned their menus around homegrown and seasonal crops.*

In spring, we ate vast quantities of greens: lettuce from our tiny garden, dandelions dug from the banks of the Miami River and our favorite – watercress from country streams. At the optimum time in spring, Daddy drove Mother and me to selected spots where we plunged our hands into icy running water and lifted out masses of wild watercress. At home, Mother fried bits of bacon and added vinegar and sugar and water to the drippings. She boiled the mixture a couple of minutes in a heavy skillet and then brought the pan to the table and poured the dressing over the watercress in a big lopsided crockery bowl. My mouth waters at the memory.

I N SUMMERTIME, MOTHER AND I HARVESTED BIG BOY TOMATOES *from vines we planted in the spring. Grocery-store tomatoes couldn't compete with the ones we grew in our backyard. The perfect tomato was one you picked on a hot summer day, washed at the spigot on the side of the house and bit into, the juices dribbling down your wrist.*

Mother and I were the planters and gatherers, and Daddy was the hunter. Late one summer night, he left the house with a pitchfork-like tool and a battery-powered light that he strapped on his forehead.

Mother and I went to bed, but were awakened hours later by Daddy; he insisted we come to the kitchen for a treat. It must have been two in the morning, but we could hear and smell the food cooking. Too excited about his catch to wait until the next day to prepare it, Daddy lopped the legs off the hapless croakers, breaded them and dropped them in hot oil. As you might guess, I did not fully appreciate my introduction to frogs' legs.

Every year around Thanksgiving, Daddy and Grandpa Newport, my maternal grandfather, cleaned their shotguns and headed for the woods. The two rarely saw eye to eye in conversation, but they had developed a camaraderie revolving around fishing and hunting. When they returned from their winter hunts, they toted canvas bags full of soft beautiful bunnies. Daddy dressed the rabbits, carefully removing the buckshot. Traditionally, he sliced off one hind foot, carefully cleaned it, neatly encased the stub with electrical tape and presented it to me as a token of good luck.

I SAVORED THE RABBIT THAT DADDY FRIED IN AN IRON SKILLET; however, I never developed a taste for the vinegary hasenpfeffer (rabbit stew) that our German-descended family considered a delicacy. Vinegar! It seemed that my mother and father used gallons every week. We had pickled beets and pickled eggs and pickled herring and pickled kidneys. I drew the line at eating kidneys, even though Mother rinsed them repeatedly before she cooked them and served them in vinegar gravy. Nothing could convince me to eat kidneys.

Pickled kidney was one of the few dishes that Daddy allowed me to pass up. The only other exception I recall was tongue. It made me gag to think of biting into an animal's tongue. Otherwise, I was expected to try every food brought to the table. My father harbored the conviction that everyone, including children, should enjoy all foods. I was not required to eat a full serving, but it was mandatory that I sample all dishes presented. I was punished if I refused: "Go to bed without your dinner!" my father would decree. I would rush off crying to my room. Occasionally, when he was in a good mood, he bribed me. Once he offered me 50 cents to chug a glass of tomato juice. I considered the viscous liquid repulsive, but I really wanted that 50 cents so I downed it without pausing.

When I became a teenager, he tried a new tactic — telling me that some day a rich gentleman would invite me to an elegant restaurant and order a gourmet meal for me. If I turned down unfamiliar foods, Daddy warned, I would not get a second date. Thus he enticed me to eat caviar (even though I knew it was fish eggs), venison (poor Bambi), sukiyaki and other foods with exotic names.

As a child, I simply accepted the idiosyncrasies of my family and didn't think it strange that my relatives nurtured live turtles in the basement until it was time to cook soup. I wasn't even disgusted by consuming meaty morsels that once were connected to my good luck charm.

In my adulthood, however, I admit that as much as I prefer the texture of the tomatoes grown in my own yard, I find it more convenient to gather the bulk of my produce from the bins at the local supermarket and consider myself fortunate to purchase poultry that has been cleaned and plucked and tidily packaged by someone else.

Soups and Salads

G REAT GRANDMA WEGHORN BOUGHT LIVE TURTLES AND HOUSED
them in tubs, feeding them until she was ready to cook them. It's
not surprising that her daughter – my Grandma Schillo –maintained
the tradition. On the morning of New Year's Eve, Grandma Schillo
started preparing her soup. I won't go into the gory details, but besides the
butchering, there was a lot of vegetable cleaning and chopping to do.

By evening, Grandma's relatives started arriving. Her brother
John Weghorn unfailingly marched directly to the massive pot on the
stove and put a big spoon down into the simmering broth, brought
it to his mouth, blew on it and made the annual pronouncement that
his sister had mastered their mother's recipe.

Soon Grandma and Grandpa's little house at 1012 Warwick Place
was bulging with every member of Uncle Johnnie and Aunt Louella's
large brood of children and grandchildren. As I took coats, Daddy and
Grandpa dispensed hot drinks to the adults and Mother offered root
beer floats to the kids. Then the men headed to the basement to play
pinochle, and the women and children crowded into the living room
to sing carols, gossip and dance the hokey-pokey.

Meanwhile, Grandma stayed in the kitchen frying fresh turtle and
stirring the soup. It was spicy and had lots of thin slices of lemon
floating on top. I never found her recipe, but I've experimented and
this combination is close to the taste I remember

No, I don't expect you to look for live turtles, but you might want to
know that some markets carry frozen turtle. Oxtails can be substituted
for a mock turtle soup. It is an unusual soup, and, to be honest, you need
to develop a taste for it. I generally passed it up at family gatherings,
but I ate more than my share of the fried turtle.

Turtle Soup Like Grandma's
(or Oxtail Soup)

3 tablespoons butter

2 pounds turtle, cut in small chunks,
   or 2 pounds oxtails
$\frac{1}{2}$ cup onion, chopped
$\frac{1}{2}$ cup celery, chopped
$\frac{1}{2}$ cup carrots, diced
1 clove garlic, minced
$\frac{1}{2}$ teaspoon ground cloves or 3 whole cloves
2 bay leaves
$\frac{1}{4}$ teaspoon allspice
3 cups beef broth
3 cups water
1 can (16 ounces) chopped tomatoes
2 tablespoons fresh parsley, chopped
1 lemon, washed and sliced thin (remove
   the seeds, but not the skin)
Salt, pepper
2 hard-boiled eggs, chopped

In a large saucepan, saute the meat in the butter until brown. Add onions, celery, carrots and cook 10 minutes. Add garlic, cloves, bay leaf, allspice, beef broth and water. Bring to a boil, remove any scum that appears and reduce to simmer. Simmer about two hours. Remove cloves and bay leaves. (If using oxtails remove them and cut the meat off. Discard the bones and return meat to pan.) Bring to a boil and add tomatoes by pushing them through a sieve into the hot soup. Add parsley and lemon and simmer 15 minutes. Add salt and pepper to taste. Ladle into bowls and garnish with chopped egg. About six servings.

Note: Oxtails tend to be fatty so I would advise you to allow two days for cooking if you use them. After simmering and removing the cloves and bay leaves, place the soup in the refrigerator over night (or at least four hours); the next morning skim all the fat off the top, and proceed with the recipe.

G REG AND JASON RAMMES WERE INSEPARABLE PALS THROUGHOUT *their elementary and high school years. Whenever I couldn't find Greg, I called the Rammes household and Jason's mother or dad knew where the two were. Whenever the Rammeses couldn't locate Jason, they dialed our house and I filled them in on the boys' whereabouts. Jason had the uncanny ability to be at our house whenever Grandma delivered her noodle soup, and we automatically set a place at the table for him.*

Grandma's Beef Noodle Soup

1 bone-in chuck roast, $2\frac{1}{2}$ to 3 pounds
    (If you cannot find a roast with a bone,
    add a couple of beef short ribs or pork
    ribs to the pot)
10 cups water
1 can (28 ounces) tomatoes
Salt, pepper

Bring roast and water to a boil in a large soup pot. Skim off the scum that rises to the top. Lower the heat and simmer two hours. Add salt and pepper to taste. Meanwhile, make the noodles.

Noodles
4 eggs
About 2 cups flour

Place flour in a deep bowl or on a lightly floured pastry board. Make a well in the center and add the eggs. Mix with hands until a ball is formed. If necessary, add small amounts of flour to form ball. Divide into four parts, and with a lightly floured rolling pin on a floured surface, roll out the dough to about $\frac{1}{4}$-inch thick. Cut with a floured sharp knife or pizza cutter into strips about 1/4-inch wide and 3 inches long. Lay the noodles flat on a clean tea towel to dry and cover with another tea towel. Allow to dry two to four hours.

Final Steps

After meat has simmered two hours, remove it from the broth and discard the fat and the bones. Set the meat aside. Press tomatoes through a fine sieve into the broth. Bring to a boil. Add the noodles and boil until tender, about 15 minutes. Return meat to the pot and reheat. Season generously with salt and pepper.

To serve, remove hot meat and cut into slices. Ladle soup into bowls. Serve catsup with the meat. This is good with a salad and thick slices of dark rye bread. If you prefer, you can cut the meat into chunks and serve it in the soup rather than on the side. About eight servings.

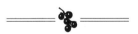

IN WINTER, MOTHER — THE COMFORT-FOOD COOK AT OUR HOUSE — *made potato soup for lunch. It was hot and milky thin with chunks of potato and half moons of celery bobbing in it. In summer, Daddy — the gourmet cook in our family — prepared an icy cold version with a fancy French name.*

Mother's Potato Soup

½ cup onion, chopped
½ cup celery, thinly sliced
3 tablespoons butter
1 teaspoon flour
3 cups potatoes, peeled and cubed
4 cups whole milk

1 teaspoon salt
1 teaspoon pepper
2 tablespoons fresh parsley, chopped
Grated cheddar cheese (optional)
3 slices bacon, fried crisp and
    crumbled (optional)

In a small skillet, sauté onion and celery in butter until vegetables are tender. Add flour and stir until blended. Remove from heat. In a saucepan, boil cubed potatoes, with water to cover, until tender. Drain and return the potatoes to the pan. Add the vegetable mixture. Stir in milk, salt, pepper and parsley. Bring to a boil; then lower heat and simmer about 10 minutes.

Ladle into bowls and top with cheddar and bacon, if you wish. If you prefer a thicker soup, remove half of it from the pan and place it in a blender or food processor for a few seconds. Return it to the remaining mixture and reheat. About four servings.

Daddy's Vichyssoise

3 cups peeled, sliced potatoes
3 cups sliced leeks, white parts only
6 cups chicken broth
1 cup half-and-half
Salt
Chopped fresh chives
Sour cream

Simmer potatoes and leeks in chicken broth until soft, about 15 to 20 minutes. Place mixture in food processor or blender and blend until smooth. Stir in half-and-half. Add salt to taste. Chill well. Serve in chilled bowls and garnish with a sprinkling of chopped chives and spoonful of sour cream. Six servings.

THIS IS THE SOUP GRANDMA MADE WHEN I WAS SICK WITH A COLD. *The aroma enticed me to breathe. If I had a sore throat as well, I also got her personal prescription: slices of fresh pineapple. Make this soup over a two-day period.*

Grandma's Chicken Rice Soup

1 small frying chicken, cut into parts (Discard organ parts or use for another purpose)
12 cups water
$\frac{1}{2}$ teaspoon garlic powder
1 teaspoon salt
$\frac{1}{2}$ teaspoon pepper
1 carrot, cut in chunks
1 onion, cut in chunks
2 ribs celery, cut in chunks
$\frac{1}{2}$ cup carrots, finely chopped
$\frac{1}{2}$ cup onions, finely chopped
$\frac{1}{2}$ cup celery, finely chopped
$\frac{1}{2}$ cup long-grain white or brown rice
2 tablespoons finely chopped parsley

Rinse chicken pieces and place in water and bring to a boil; skim off the scum as it begins to boil. Add garlic powder, salt, pepper and chunks of carrot, onion and celery. Reduce heat to low and simmer, partially covered, about one hour, or until meat is tender and about to fall off the bone. Cool and place in refrigerator over night.

The next day, discard the fat that has formed on the top. Remove skin and bones from chicken and cut chicken meat into bite-sized pieces. Set aside. Heat the broth and strain it through a fine sieve, discarding the vegetables. Return broth to a boil and add finely chopped vegetables and rice. Reduce heat; simmer about 40 minutes; then return chicken to pan along with parsley. Simmer another 10 minutes. Add extra salt and pepper to taste. About 10 servings.

MOTHER USED ONLY FRESH VEGETABLES IN HER SOUP, BUT I AM *satisfied that my shortcuts do not compromise the flavor. This is another two-day process.*

Mother's Beef Vegetable Soup

2 tablespoons shortening or olive oil
3 pound bone-in chuck roast (If you cannot find a roast with a bone, add one pound of beef shortribs or pork spareribs to the pot.)
12 cups water
1 medium onion, cut in chunks
2 carrots, cut in chunks
2 ribs celery, cut in chunks
2 bay leaves
1 medium onion, coarsely chopped
2 cans (14 ounces each) beef broth
1 can (14$\frac{1}{2}$ ounces) tomatoes, diced or crushed
$\frac{1}{2}$ teaspoon fresh minced garlic
1 package (14 ounces) frozen mixed vegetables
$\frac{1}{2}$ cup frozen lima beans
2 cups cabbage, shredded
$\frac{1}{2}$ cup frozen corn kernels
Salt and pepper to taste

Brown the roast (and bones) and onion in the shortening in a large pot. Add water, other chunks of vegetables and bay leaves. Bring to a boil and then lower the heat and simmer about two hours, partially covered, until the meat is tender. Remove the bay leaves. Refrigerate overnight.

The next day remove the fat that has formed on the top and remove the meat (and bones). Discard fat and bones, cut meat into bite-sized pieces and set aside. Heat the broth until warm, remove the vegetables and strain the broth into another large pot, being sure to discard the bay leaves. Return to the stove. Add beef broth and bring to a boil. Add chopped onion, tomatoes, garlic, mixed vegetables, lima beans, cabbage and corn. Simmer 20 minutes. Add the meat and simmer another 10 minutes. Season to taste. About 12 servings.

M Y ALL-TIME FAVORITE COOKBOOK IS ONE THAT NO ONE ELSE *owns. It's called* Jill's Joy of Cooking. *The little volume was presented to Jim and me by Jill and Robin Franz when they were teenagers. The girls copied their favorite recipes, prepared the dishes, photographed the results and bound the book as a Christmas gift. It serves as a sentimental reminder of the years I lived on Lonsdale Avenue in Oakwood next to the Franz's.*

This soup recipe is from my treasured book. Bill, Laurie, Robin and Jill delivered a pot of the vegetarian chili to our home after Mother's funeral. We since have taken it to other bereaved families.

Franz's Vegetarian Chili

1 large onion, coarsely chopped
1 tablespoon vegetable oil
1 can (28 ounces) whole tomatoes, undrained

and coarsely chopped
⅔ cup chunky picante sauce or salsa
1½ teaspoons ground cumin
1 teaspoon salt
½ teaspoon dried basil
1 can (15 ounces) black beans
1 green bell pepper, cut into ½-inch chunks
1 red bell pepper, cut into ½-inch chunks
1 large yellow squash, cut into ½-inch chunks
Optional toppings: chopped fresh cilantro, sour
    cream, shredded cheese or hot cooked rice

In a soup pot, cook onion in oil until tender, about three minutes. Add tomatoes, picante sauce, cumin, salt and basil. Cover. Simmer five minutes. Stir in the beans, peppers and squash. Cover and simmer until vegetables are tender, about 15 minutes. Ladle into bowls. Top as you wish. About four servings.

COLUMBUS, OHIO, FRIENDS CHERYL AND TOM BAXTER AND THEIR *three daughters opened coolers full of homemade food when they arrived at our Lake Erie cottage. Our favorite offering was this chicken soup – a good choice for summer days. Season it to your taste, but don't leave out the cilantro – it provides a zesty touch.*

Cheryl's Tortilla Soup

2 medium onions, chopped
4 cloves garlic, mashed
1 can (7 ounces) green chilies, chopped
1 tablespoon olive oil
8 cups chicken broth
4 boneless chicken breasts, chopped
1 can (15 ounces) tomatoes, chopped
Cumin to taste (½ teaspoon more or less)

Cayenne pepper to taste (optional)
Sour cream
Chopped cilantro
2 or 3 tortillas, cut into strips and fried in a
small amount of oil until browned

Saute onions, garlic and chilies in olive oil. Heat chicken broth to boiling and add sautéed vegetables along with the chopped chicken and tomatoes. Return to boil; then lower heat and simmer 30 minutes. Add seasonings to taste. Ladle into bowls and garnish with chopped cilantro, dollops of sour cream and crispy tortilla strips. Eight servings.

KATHRIN RUDLAND, A FRIEND IN THE GREENSBORO (GEORGIA) *Writers' Guild, is a talented poet, devoted gardener and splendid cook. Enjoy her poetic reverie and make her soup at summer's end when homegrown tomatoes are at their best.*

Kathrin's Gazpacho

$\frac{1}{2}$ cup FRESH herbs (basil, chives, oregano,
marjoram, parsley and chervil, or whatever
is available fresh)
2 cloves garlic, skins removed and pressed
in garlic press
$\frac{1}{4}$ cup extra-virgin olive oil
Juice of 1 fresh lemon
3 cups meat stock or beef broth
$2\frac{1}{2}$ pounds vine-ripened tomatoes, peeled,
seeded and finely chopped
1 large Vidalia onion or other sweet onion,
quartered and sliced paper-thin
2 stalks celery, strings removed and sliced
paper-thin

2 medium seedless cucumbers, peeled and
    sliced paper-thin
Salt and cracked pepper to taste
Optional toppings: croutons and sour cream

Chop herbs and mash with garlic. Place herbs in
a large bowl and slowly add olive oil and lemon
juice until a thick mash is formed. Stir in beef broth
and add tomatoes, onion, celery and cucumbers.
Season with salt and pepper to taste. Chill at least
four hours or overnight until thoroughly chilled
and flavors have ripened. Serve in chilled goblets
or mugs topped with croutons or dollops of sour
cream, if desired. Four servings.

Celebration

By Kathrin Rudland

There is a kind of harmony in it,
this celebration of our summer garden,
as we seed and dice plump, ruby-red tomatoes,
cut paper-thin slices of celery, onion, cucumber
rub together olive oil, lemon, garlic,
add a handful of freshly washed herbs,
drizzle in rich, clear meat stock
then stir together in a broad, deep bowl
and chill and chill
until the flavors satisfy and ripen one another
in some sort of liquid melody.

As we await our meal in the cool of the evening
we think of the patient seedlings
that grew with the season's days
into our harvest of lush vegetables

so that we could gather them together
and toast the earth, the soft rains, and the summer sky
with icy goblets of gazpacho.

WHEN DADDY SERVED IN THE NAVY DURING WORLD WAR II, *Mother and I lived in a converted garage a few doors away from Great Grandma Weghorn. Although I was only six years old when we lived near her, I remember the touch of her big hands on my little ones as she taught me to hold a crochet needle and to make a chain stitch. We sat on wicker furniture on her front porch for the lessons. Two of her wicker chairs are on my porch in Georgia.*

She also had an influence on Mother's cooking and taught her to make this salad.

Great Grandma's Wilted Watercress

2 bunches of watercress, or 1 head leaf lettuce
½ sweet onion, sliced in thin rings
8 slices bacon
6 tablespoons bacon grease
¾ cup cider vinegar
⅓ cup water
4 tablespoons sugar
½ teaspoon salt
¼ teaspoon pepper

Clean the watercress or lettuce and tear into bite-sized pieces. Place in a deep bowl with the onion rings. Chill this in the refrigerator while preparing the dressing.

Fry bacon very crisp in a skillet. Remove bacon and reserve six tablespoons of the drippings in the skillet. Heat the drippings and add vinegar, water, sugar, salt and pepper. Heat to boiling, stirring until sugar dissolves. Crumble bacon into bits and combine with lettuce and onion. Pour hot dressing over salad mixture and toss well. Eat it while it's warm. Serves four.

YOUNG CHILDREN TODAY ARE LIKELY TO REQUEST A MCDONALD'S *hamburger and fries for a birthday meal. But I requested roast veal with au gratin noodles and this grated coleslaw. Prepare this several hours before serving.*

Grandma's Sweet and Sour Slaw

1 small head cabbage, grated on large holes of
    a hand grater or chopped fine in a
    food processor
1 large onion, grated or chopped fine
1 small green pepper, chopped fine

Combine cabbage, onion and green pepper and
    chill while preparing dressing.

Dressing
1 cup cider vinegar
1 cup sugar or no-calorie sweetener, such
    as Splenda
$\frac{1}{4}$ cup vegetable oil
1 teaspoon salt

Combine vinegar, sugar, oil and salt in a medium-sized saucepan and bring to a boil. Lower the heat and simmer two to three minutes, until sugar is dissolved. Cool. Pour cooled dressing over cabbage mixture. Stir well. Refrigerate at least four hours or overnight before serving. Eight servings.

The home of Jim's youth bulged with family and friends in *need of shelter. Cousin Charlie stayed for years. Cousin Clyde was there off and on, and "Aunt" Prissie was a long-term resident.*

When Beverly and Jim were married, they continued the tradition. Cousins came to stay now and then, and Jim's elementary school buddy Ken Burke moved into the household for a while.

Jay Kyne, a University of Dayton student, originally came to the couple's Springboro, Ohio, farm to help with the horses and earn college funds. The family became so attached to the charismatic young man that they "adopted" him as a surrogate son, and he continued to live under their roof for a couple of years after graduation.

Jay and his wife Cindy Fox now reside in their own cozy home in Raleigh, North Carolina, but they remain family and join us for holidays and milestone events.

Jay does not eat mayonnaise; this is his recipe for slaw.

Jay's No-Mayo Summer Slaw

1 bag (12 to 16 ounces) angel hair cabbage slaw
¾ cup extra virgin olive oil
¼ cup apple cider vinegar
½ to 1 teaspoon garlic powder
1 teaspoon celery seed or poppy seed
½ teaspoon salt
½ teaspoon pepper
¼ cup sugar

Mix all ingredients and chill an hour or so before mealtime. About 6 servings.

Grandma canned this green tomato relish every fall. We *ate it on hotdogs and hamburgers and as a side to pork chops. On my list of life "to do's" is to learn canning methods and prepare this recipe. It makes seven or eight pints so you will need seven or eight pint-sized canning jars.*

A note on turmeric: it's a spice used in pickles and relishes to add both color and flavor. If you want to learn about spices, check the McCormick spice company's website; it's terrific. According to the company, Marco Polo made note of turmeric on his China travels, comparing it to saffron. You can look up saffron, too, at this site, and you will learn why the stuff is so expensive.

Make this over a two-day period.

Grandma's Piccalilli (Green Tomato Relish)

Vegetables

10 to 12 medium-sized green tomatoes
10 to 12 medium-sized green peppers
8 medium-sized yellow onions
1 medium-sized cabbage
$\frac{1}{2}$ cup salt

Cut the vegetables into pieces; then coarsely grind them. Grandma used a hand grinder; you can use a food processor. Add salt and stir. Cover the mixture with plastic wrap and let stand in the refrigerator overnight. The next day, drain and rinse with cold water. Squeeze remaining water out with your hands. Then prepare syrup.

Syrup

6 cups sugar
1 teaspoon celery seed
1 teaspoon mustard seed
4 cups white vinegar
1 cup water
1 teaspoon ground turmeric

Combine sugar, celery seed, mustard seed, white vinegar and water in a large pan and bring the mixture to a boil, stirring frequently. Add the vegetables, lower the heat and simmer 15 minutes. Then add the turmeric and simmer another five minutes. Spoon the hot mixture into seven or eight hot, sterilized pint-size canning jars. Place the caps on and process 15 minutes in a boiling water bath. Make sure your seal is good. You may want to read up on canning before you tackle this recipe. Makes seven or eight pints.

I DOUBT THAT MOTHER EVER VISITED THE NEW YORK HOTEL THAT *introduced this dish in the late 1800s, but she was infatuated with the salad and made it frequently in the fall. You can use no-fat or low-fat mayo for a lower-calorie version. Incidentally, the Waldorf hotel's original recipe called for only three ingredients – apples, celery and mayonnaise.*

Mother's Waldorf Salad

2 large red apples, diced (leave peel on)
1 tablespoon lemon juice
$\frac{1}{2}$ cup celery, chopped
$\frac{1}{4}$ cup raisins
$\frac{1}{4}$ cup walnuts, chopped
$\frac{1}{4}$ cup mayonnaise
1 teaspoon sugar
Red seedless grapes (for garnish)

Combine apples and lemon juice. Add celery, raisins, walnuts, mayonnaise and sugar. Mix well and chill at least two hours. Serve on a bed of lettuce and garnish with seedless grapes and a dollop of mayonnaise. Four servings.

POPULAR IN THE 1950S, THIS DISH IS A DESSERT MASQUERADING AS *a salad. There are many versions. This one is from Grandma's recipe file, passed on to her by a friend named Irma Fick.*

Grandma and Irma's 7-Up Salad

2 packages (3 ounces each) lemon gelatin
2 cups boiling water
2 cups 7-Up
1 cup crushed pineapple, drained; reserve juice
1 cup miniature marshmallows
2 large bananas, sliced
$\frac{1}{2}$ cup sugar
1 egg
1 tablespoon flour
1 cup reserved pineapple juice
2 tablespoons butter
1 cup whipped topping, such as Cool Whip
    (Grandma used Dream Whip)
Grated cheddar cheese (optional)
Finely chopped walnuts (optional)

Dissolve gelatin in boiling water; then add 7-up. Chill until almost set, about 30 minutes. Add pineapple, marshmallows and banana slices. Pour into 10x13-inch pan and return to refrigerator.

Meanwhile in a saucepan, combine sugar, egg, flour and pineapple juice. Cook on medium heat until thickened. Remove from heat and add butter. Cool. Mix whipped topping into cooled filling in saucepan. Spread this mixture over top of chilled gelatin mixture. If desired, sprinkle walnuts and cheese over top. Twelve to 16 servings.

D URING JENNI'S TEEN YEARS, I OFTEN FOUND HALF A BOWL OF *this salad in the refrigerator when I got home from work. She ate half of it as soon as she made it. Deep in my recipe box, I discovered these instructions written in green ink on her high school notebook paper.*

Jenni's Macaroni Salad

1 cup uncooked elbow macaroni
½ cup mayonnaise
1 carrot, diced
3 hard-boiled eggs, sliced
½ small yellow onion, thinly sliced
1 teaspoon lemon juice
1 ½ teaspoons sugar
Salt and pepper to taste

Cook macaroni according to package directions. In a large bowl, combine mayonnaise, carrot, eggs, onion, lemon juice, sugar and salt and pepper. Add drained, cooked macaroni and mix well. Chill. Four servings.

I KNEW MY DAUGHTER WAS ALL GROWN UP WHEN SHE INVITED ME TO *a dinner party at her Boston apartment. She had graduated from making macaroni salad to preparing this sophisticated summer salad that she artfully layered on a large platter. Her guests included Ned and their best friends, Sarah and Dave Cuthill. I had never tasted Gorgonzola cheese before that day, and since then it has been my favorite cheese for salad.*

Jenni's Dinner Party Salad

3 large yellow or orange sweet peppers,
    thinly sliced into rings
3 large red tomatoes, sliced

1 small red onion, thinly sliced into rings
12 ounces fresh spinach leaves
²⁄₃ cup Gorgonzola cheese, crumbled

Bring a small amount of water, a half cup or so, to boil in a large skillet. Cook pepper rings one or two minutes in the boiling water; drain and chill. Cover a platter with the spinach. Arrange tomato, onion slices and pepper rings in an overlapping manner over the spinach. Sprinkle crumbled cheese on top. Dribble chilled dressing on the salad. Makes about six side salads.

Dressing

4 tablespoons olive oil
4 tablespoons white balsamic vinegar or white
    wine vinegar
1 tablespoon sliced green onion
2 teaspoons chopped fresh basil
1 teaspoon sugar
½ teaspoon Dijon mustard
⅛ teaspoon pepper

Combine oil, vinegar, onion, basil, sugar, mustard and pepper in a cruet or plastic container. Cover. Shake well and chill.

IN 1978, ARNOLD ROSENFELD, EDITOR IN CHIEF OF THE Dayton Daily News, *offered me the job of Lifestyle editor of the newspaper. I wanted to accept, but confessed that I was not sure I could handle it. I was fearful of the computers. All editing was done on a computer and my computer literacy was rudimentary at best. He assured me that he had learned to operate computers, and if he could learn, so could I. He said he would simply ask the assistant editor to teach me how to do that part of my job. Then he introduced me to Carol Muller*

— who, patiently and graciously — taught her new boss how to master electronic editing.

Carol's off-the-job passion was reading cookbooks, and it was from her that I, too, acquired my attachment to cookbooks. Carol, who now lives in San Jose, California, is an excellent cook. This is one of her memorable recipes.

Carol's Spinach Salad with Hot Dressing

12 ounces torn spinach greens
$\frac{1}{4}$ pound fresh mushrooms, sliced
$\frac{1}{2}$ red onion, sliced
$\frac{1}{2}$ cup vegetable oil
$\frac{1}{2}$ cup sugar or no-calorie sweetener, such
  as Splenda
$\frac{1}{4}$ cup catsup
2 tablespoons Worcestershire

Combine spinach, mushrooms and onion in a salad bowl. In a small saucepan, mix together oil, sugar, catsup and Worcestershire and heat slowly until sugar melts. Pour over vegetables and serve immediately. Serves four.

CAROL ALSO INTRODUCED ME TO TABBOULEH. IT IS A REFRESHING *change from a tossed salad. Make it a day before serving to allow the flavors to fully develop. Bulgur, a Middle Eastern staple, is parboiled wheat. There are many versions of this dish, but this is the combination I prefer.*

Tabbouleh

1 cup bulgur
1 cup boiling water

4 green onions, chopped, white and green parts
1½ cups fresh parsley, stems removed, chopped
1 cup chopped cherry tomatoes (or plum
    tomatoes)
¼ cup fresh mint, finely chopped
1 can (2½ ounces) black olives, sliced and drained
¼ cup olive oil
½ teaspoon dried oregano
⅓ cup lemon juice
¼ teaspoon garlic powder
1 teaspoon salt
Dash pepper

Put the bulgur in a small bowl and pour one cup
boiling water over it. Let it stand for half an hour
and then pour it into a sieve to drain it thoroughly.
Place drained bulgur in a large bowl; add and mix
the onions, parsley, tomatoes, mint and olives. In a
separate small bowl, combine the olive oil, oregano,
lemon juice, garlic powder, salt and pepper. Pour over
the mixed vegetables and toss. Refrigerate at least
three hours or overnight. Six to eight servings.

JIM'S OHIO STATE UNIVERSITY COLLEAGUE, DR. ERNIE MAZZAFERRI,
and his wife Florence are unparalleled hosts. Ernie is accomplished
at the grill, and Florence creates gourmet dishes in her dream kitchen.
In their home in Gainesville, Florida, she opened our meal with this
salad. It was perfect with the salmon that Ernie prepared. Note that
the dressing needs to be chilled overnight.

Florence's Spinach Salad with Onion Dressing

12 ounces fresh spinach
1 cup stuffing croutons, such as Pepperidge Farm

⅓ pound bacon, cooked and crumbled
2 hard-cooked eggs, sliced

Dressing
1 medium red onion, chopped fine
⅔ cup sugar (no-calorie sweetener can be used
    satisfactorily)
1 teaspoon salt
1 teaspoon celery seed
½ teaspoon pepper
3 teaspoons mustard
⅓ cup white wine vinegar
⅓ cup vegetable oil

Place all dressing ingredients in a blender or food
processor and blend well. Chill overnight. Arrange
salad ingredients on platter and toss with dressing
at serving time. Four servings.

A T A CHURCH POTLUCK YEARS AGO, I TASTED THIS SALAD, BUT
*failed to identify who brought it. I tinkered until I produced this
dish that closely resembles the original.*

Joan's Spinach Salad with Mayonnaise Dressing

10 ounces fresh spinach
½ medium red onion, thinly sliced
1 cup fresh mushrooms, sliced
⅓ cup mayonnaise
⅓ cup sour cream
½ teaspoon garlic powder
2 hard-cooked eggs, sliced
½ teaspoon salt
Dash of pepper

4 bacon slices, fried crisp and crumbled

In a large bowl, combine spinach, onion slices and mushrooms. In a small bowl, mix mayonnaise, sour cream, garlic powder, salt, pepper and sliced eggs. Pour mayonnaise mixture over spinach mixture and mix. Chill about an hour. At serving time, garnish with bacon. Four servings.

WHEN THE *Dayton Daily News* LIFESTYLE STAFF GOT TOGETHER *for fun, there was good food as well. Staff secretary Sharry Anderson — the most orderly person I knew — sometimes brought this tidy, tasty salad. You can make it in quantities to suit your need. Present it in a clear, deep glass bowl or a trifle dish to show off the layers.*

Sharry's Layered Salad

Leaf, romaine or bibb lettuce, torn into bite-
    sized pieces
Sliced celery
Cherry tomatoes, halved
Chopped onions
Shredded cheddar
Crumbled crisp bacon
Frozen baby peas, thawed
Mayonnaise
Hard-cooked eggs, chopped

Layer bottom of bowl with lettuce. Then layer celery, tomatoes, lettuce, onions, lettuce, mayonnaise, lettuce, cheddar, lettuce, bacon, lettuce, peas, lettuce. Cover with a layer of mayonnaise and top with chopped eggs.

Old-fashioned potlucks get my vote for the best kind of party. *Jim and I frequently hosted them at our Worthington, Ohio, home during the mid-1990s. One evening staffers from "The James" cancer hospital arrived with their specialties. Robin Wyatt's salad was a hit with the guests. Robin brought each group of ingredients in separate plastic containers and tossed them in a big salad bowl at mealtime.*

Robin's Ramen Noodle Salad

1 bunch Napa cabbage (Chinese cabbage),
    chopped
6 to 8 green onions, sliced
2 packages ramen noodles, crushed
$\frac{1}{2}$ cup sesame seeds (yes, that's a lot of sesame
    seeds)
1 small package (2 or 3 ounces) slivered almonds
1 stick butter or margarine (you can reduce
    the amount to half a stick if you wish)
1 cup vegetable oil
1 cup sugar (no-calorie sweetener is acceptable)
$\frac{1}{2}$ cup cider vinegar
Salt, pepper to taste

Mix cabbage and onions together in a large bowl. Cover and place in refrigerator. Saute noodles, sesame seeds and nuts in butter until light brown. In a medium bowl, mix oil, sugar, vinegar, salt and pepper. Chill. When ready to serve, mix cabbage and onions with noodle mixture and dressing. Serve immediately.

This salad does not keep; noodles soften after a while. If you wish to make ahead, keep the three mixtures separate and chilled; then combine at serving time. Ten to 12 side servings.

DR. EARL METZ, WHO WAS JIM'S FELLOW ONCOLOGIST AT "THE *James" cancer hospital, is married to the woman we consider one of the best cooks in Columbus. We frequently requested her recipes and she always generously shared them. This salad is a good way to fulfill your daily requirements for cruciferous vegetables.*

Mary Alice's Sunny Salad

5 cups each broccoli and cauliflower, chopped
2 cups shredded sharp cheddar cheese
½ cup chopped onions
1 cup salad dressing, such as Hellman's or
    Kraft (light is okay)
½ cup sugar or no-calorie sweetener, such
    as Splenda
2 tablespoons red wine vinegar or cider vinegar
½ cup raisins
½ cup crumbled, crisp bacon
½ cup roasted sunflower kernels

Combine broccoli, cauliflower, cheese and onions in a large bowl. In a smaller bowl, mix together salad dressing, sugar and vinegar. Combine the vegetable mixture with the dressing in a large bowl and chill at least an hour. Before serving, mix in the raisins, bacon and sunflower seeds. Six to eight servings.

CHERRY TREES SPAN THE HORIZON IN THE SPRING NEAR SUSAN *AND Michael Craig's home in Leland, Michigan. So it shouldn't have come as a surprise when we opened our Christmas package to find dried cherries. There were eight pounds of them! We simmered those cherries in oatmeal, sprinkled them in salads and baked them in muffins. They are a good substitute for raisins in a traditional broccoli salad.*

Broccoli Salad with Cherries

4 cups fresh broccoli, cut into small pieces
¼ cup red onion, minced
1 cup dried cherries
½ cup roasted sunflower kernels
½ cup mayonnaise
1 tablespoon cider vinegar
2 tablespoons sugar
4 slices bacon, fried crisp and crumbled

In a large bowl, combine broccoli, onion, cherries and sunflower kernels. In a small bowl, combine mayonnaise, vinegar and sugar. Pour dressing over vegetable mixture and toss. Chill. Before serving, add bacon crumbles. Six to eight servings.

CUCUMBERS WITH SOUR CREAM SERVED ON A BED OF LEAF LETTUCE *make a quick, low-cal salad if you use reduced-fat sour cream. This was familiar fare in the Schillo household throughout my childhood. If you grow the cucumbers yourself, leave the peel on. However, if you buy them at the grocery, I'd suggest you remove the peel; often they are waxed to protect them during transportation.*

Creamy Cucumbers

One cucumber
½ cup reduced-fat sour cream
1 tablespoon cider vinegar
Lettuce
Salt, pepper

Peel cucumber and slice into thin rounds. In a small bowl, combine sour cream and vinegar and add salt to taste. Pour over sliced cucumber and mix thoroughly. Chill. At serving time, place on a bed of lettuce and garnish with freshly ground pepper. Two or three servings.

*I*F WE DIDN'T HAVE SOUR CREAM ON HAND, MOTHER MADE A SIMPLE *vinegar dressing for the cucumbers that grew in our garden. Cucumbers are rich in Vitamin C. The ancient Greeks and Romans believed they had powers to heal the skin; today we see many hand lotions that are cucumber "flavored."*

Marinated Cucumbers and Onions

One cucumber
1 medium sweet onion, such as Vidalia,
    sliced very thin
½ cup white wine vinegar or white balsamic
    vinegar
1 or 2 packets sugar substitute, such as Equal
½ teaspoon salt
Dash pepper

Peel cucumber and slice into thin rounds. Peel onion, slice very thin and separate into rings. Mix in medium bowl. In a small bowl, combine vinegar, sugar substitute, salt and pepper. Pour over vegetables. Chill before serving. Two or three servings.

*P*ROVIDENCE BEAMED DOWN ON US WHEN WAYNE AND KAREN BAIN *left Cincinnati and moved in next door to our Great Waters home in Georgia. We go to movies, watch TV, play golf and shop together, and seldom does a week go by that we don't share a meal or two together.*

Wayne is a topnotch grill chef and chili maker, among other talents. Karen's cooking skills, however, were limited when they moved here. (I trust she doesn't mind my telling you that.) But over the years, she has developed a long list of specialties. One is this salad, which is among my Top Three all-time favorites. Sometimes she serves it as a main course – and it is worthy of that. You can top it with grilled chicken slices, if you like.

She dishes it up in oversized bowls created by Jerry and Kathy Chappelle, the couple who owns Happy Valley Pottery located in a back-roads spot near Watkinsville. Karen introduced us to Happy Valley and now we take all our house guests there. They tend to be leery when Jim and I drive them into the country and lead them to a funky collection of ramshackle buildings. But they never fail to be impressed when they see the tables lined with pottery and glass pieces made by local artisans. It's a special day when Jerry is there to show us the kiln and talk about his work, but we have been there when there wasn't a soul on the property except us. In cases like that, we simply leave the money for our purchases in a designated pot. A calculator is provided along with instructions on how to compute tax. The honor system is alive in rural Georgia, a place where neighborliness thrives.

Karen's Cashew Salad

1 cup tiny frozen peas, thawed
1 cup cashews
1 cup shredded mozzarella cheese
6 cups iceberg or romaine lettuce, chopped

Layer ingredients on a large platter or in a large, chilled salad bowl.

Dressing
$\frac{3}{4}$ cup sugar or no-calorie sweetener, such as Splenda
1 teaspoon dry mustard
1 teaspoon onion, finely chopped
1 teaspoon poppy seeds
Pinch of salt

1 cup vegetable oil
½ cup cider vinegar

In a cruet or small bowl, combine sugar, mustard, onion, poppy seeds and salt. Add oil and vinegar and whisk or shake until blended. Chill several hours. At serving time, toss with lettuce mixture. Six to eight side servings.

On New Year's Eve on Pickerel Lake in Michigan, diners *make way through snowy depths in Nancy and Dale Hines' neighborhood. The three-stop progressive dinner party starts with appetizers and cocktails at one home, moves on to the next house for entrees and to the final house for desserts, games and a jubilant welcome to the New Year. Nancy served this festive salad one year, garnishing each individual dish with snips of evergreen and frozen cranberries.*

Nancy's Cranberry Salad

2 cups boiling water
2 packages (3 ounces each) cherry gelatin
1 can (15 ounces) crushed pineapple with juice,
    chilled
1 can (16 ounces) whole cranberry sauce
8 ounces sour cream

Dissolve gelatin in boiling water. Add chilled pineapple with the juices. Stir in cranberry sauce. Chill for about 30 minutes, until it begins to gel. Stir in sour cream and pour into a nine-inch square pan. Chill several hours. Cut into squares and garnish as desired. Nine servings.

M Y ARTERIES TENSE WHEN I THINK OF MY FATHER'S FAVORITE *salad: an iceberg lettuce wedge with rich bleu cheese dressing topped with chunks of bleu cheese and a generous handful of crumbled bacon. While Jim also loves this combination, he didn't complain when I substituted this "skinny" dressing on a wedge, sprinkled cheese on top and dropped some artificial bacon bits on the dressing. Chopped green onions are a nice added touch.*

Wedge Salad with Skinny Dressing

8 ounces low-fat cottage cheese
½ cup low-fat buttermilk
1 ounce crumbled blue cheese
4 wedges of iceberg lettuce
1 ounce crumbled blue cheese
4 teaspoons bacon bits
4 teaspoons sliced green onions

Place cottage cheese, buttermilk and one ounce blue cheese in a blender and blend thoroughly. Chill at least two hours. To serve, place wedges on individual salad plates, spoon dressing over them and garnish with crumbled cheese, bacon bits and sliced onions. Four servings.

"W E LOVE A PARTY...WE ALWAYS WILL...BECAUSE A PARTY GIVES US *such a thrill!" My Chi Omega sisters sang that song when we were students at Ohio University from 1959-1963. In July, 2004, we 60-something "girls" crawled into Donna Simpson Johnston's teepee and fired up our voices with as much enthusiasm as ever. For a few joyful days, Donna's Cody, Wyoming, ranch was our refuge where we relived the sweet refrains of our maidenhood.*

At lunch, back in the ranch house, Donna offered us this unusual potato salad. She also dished up "Sloppy Sam's" (made with meat from poor Sam whose massive taxidermied head stared down upon us from above the mantel). Unlike conventional potato salads, the potatoes in this recipe are mashed, not cubed.

One of the ingredients, Durkee's Famous Sauce, was a staple in Grandma's pantry. She regularly used it as a sandwich spread. I couldn't find it in local groceries so I turned to the Internet. The Durkee website explained that the sauce was created in 1857 and was carried west in covered wagons by the pioneers. It is believed that Mary Todd Lincoln served it to Abraham Lincoln during the Civil War years.

I ended up ordering the sauce from the Vermont Country Store website. If you are a child of the '50s as I am, you will enjoy a nostalgic visit on this site. The products of our youth are all available, from Bosco Syrup and Horlick's Malted Milk Tablets to 1955 Super Tournament Wood Yo-Yos.

Donna's Sweet Potato Salad

4 large sweet potatoes, cooked and mashed,
    about 5 cups
¼ cup chopped green onions
3 or 4 hard-boiled eggs, chopped
1 can (10 ounces) crushed pineapple,
    drained (optional)
½ cup Durkee's dressing
About ⅓ cup salad dressing, such as
    Miracle Whip
1 tablespoon cider vinegar
1 tablespoon sugar
Garlic salt to taste

In a large bowl, mix all ingredients. Chill well before serving. About eight servings.

The T-Bone Kid

WIND UP...PITCH...THUMP! WIND UP...PITCH...THUMP! YOUNG *Jimmy Ungerleider played alone in the alley behind the aging buildings. He approached the "mound," adopted the proper stance and pitched to the wall. He could almost hear the umpire bellow: "Strrrike one! Strrrike two!"*

Most afternoons after classes at St. Agnes Elementary School in Dayton, the seventh-grader biked to his Salem Avenue home across from Grace Methodist Church, changed clothes and wandered down the street to check in with his parents at work before heading to the alley to perfect his pitching.

When he bored of his solitary game, he ventured into Hy Lichtman's corner drugstore and paged through the Captain Marvel and Superman comic books until the proprietor shooed him out. Finally, he returned next door to Sully's Restaurant where his parents were preparing to greet the early diners.

One afternoon, sweaty and thirsty from his pitching practice, Jim bolted into the restaurant and seated himself next to his mother at the bar. In front of her was an enticing glass full of clear, cool liquid. Before she could protest, he grabbed it, took a gulp – and gasped. Not water. Gin. His first martini.

Monday through Thursday in the 1950s, the youngster dined in his parents' establishment on a choice-cut T-bone steak prepared by broiler master Eddie Haynes. With it, a salad, baked potato (with butter and sour cream) and vegetable of the day.

On Fridays, his mother Florence (affectionately called "Flossie" by friends) protected her son's standing in the Catholic Church by insisting that he eat halibut, a dish he intensely disliked. He much preferred meat.

JIM FREQUENTLY ATE HIS MEALS IN THE TINY KITCHEN WITH EDDIE *the cook. But some nights Jim's father Lou asked a regular patron – often a physician or professor dining alone -- if his young son could join him. The adult conversation at these dinners made a lifelong impression on the youth and influenced Jim to settle on medicine as a profession.*

JACK, LEFT, AND JIM HELP FLOSSIE CELEBRATE HER 70TH BIRTHDAY

Both Jim and his older brother Jack had responsibilities at the restaurant. Jim often prepared the menus. He layered white paper with carbons between the pages and typed the daily specials. Then he slid each sheet into a sheath of plastic. A steak dinner with salad, potato, vegetable, roll and butter was $2.50. Lower-priced meals included fish, fried chicken and city chicken, which, strangely enough, was not chicken at all; it was a combination of veal and pork.

Lou Ungerleider painstakingly kept the books at Sully's, which was named for former owner Jim Sullivan. He also ordered supplies and managed the employees. Flossie was the upfront member of the partnership. The outgoing hostess was friendly in her manner and flashy in her dress. She hovered over the presentation of the foods,

LOU AND FLOSSIE, CENTER, SURROUNDED BY FRIENDS IN SULLY'S

ensuring that each meal delivered to the table was a feast for the eyes as well as the stomach.

Occasionally, Flossie cooked. Her specialty dessert was a distinctive cheesecake. Unlike round, flat New York cheesecakes, hers was high and had a hole in the middle. She baked it in an angel food cake pan, which was placed in a moderately hot oven for an hour; afterward it stayed in the oven with the heat turned off and the door ajar. This dessert was sinfully rich; to make a single cake, she used five large packages of cream cheese, a half dozen eggs and a heavy dose of whipping cream. The crust was made of zwieback, (those hard cookies babies teethe on) instead of traditional graham cracker crumbs.

FLOSSIE RESERVED MOST OF HER PERSONAL COOKING FOR SUMMER *days at a rental cottage at Indian Lake, where the "family" vacationed every year. This so-called "family" requires some* explanation. *The core group consisted of four people – Jim, his brother Jack and their parents. But also living under the same roof at most times during the year were:*

Charlie Cooper – Flossie's cousin, orphaned as a child and housed by various family members over the years.

"Aunt" Prissie – whose full name was Priscilla Alden. She professed to be a descendant of the woman we read about in history books. Flossie befriended her when Prissie worked in the beauty salon of the May & Company department store in Cleveland. Once she invited Prissie to come to the Ungerleider home for the weekend. Prissie came with her bags and never left.

Frank Harris – a gentle man who performed maintenance tasks in both the restaurant and Ungerleider household. Jim adored Frank, who was wise and kind, and memorialized him by designating "Harris" as son Matt's middle name.

"Little Clyde" – the son of "Big Clyde," Flossie's brother. He lived intermittently with the Ungerleiders. He worked at Sully's, too, sometimes as a bartender and sometimes as maitre d'.

T HESE EIGHT PEOPLE COMPRISED THE ENTOURAGE THAT MADE *the summer pilgrimage to Indian Lake. Lou annually rented a trailer and crammed it with the silverware, pots and pans, linens and other furnishings that Flossie considered indispensable for summer entertaining.*

On weekends, the Ungerleider clan shared this cottage with friends who made the drive from Dayton or Springfield (where Lou and Flossie later purchased a restaurant). They fished, swam and cruised the lake on the "Jim-Jack," a classic wooden Chris Craft inboard motorboat. Jack, because he was the older brother, usually took the helm, but in moments of generosity, he allowed his eager younger sibling to fulfill the captain's role.

I N THE EVENINGS, FLOSSIE SERVED GUESTS HEARTY HOME-COOKED *meals of roasted meats, cabbage rolls, hamburgers and ham. Later, she cleared the table and brought out playing cards for lively hands of poker and Lou's favorite, gin rummy. On Monday mornings, Lou reluctantly made the hour-and-a-half journey back to Dayton* to resume control of the restaurant. Flossie stayed behind to bask in three months of leisure with her sons.

Sully's restaurant closed decades ago. Lou and Flossie are gone, too. The brothers live on opposite sides of the country — but both are immersed in lifestyles that are not at all surprising when you understand their past. Big families, loyal friends and powerful boats are still their passions — passions they celebrate together, often with a chilled martini in hand and a thick steak sizzling on the grill.

Entrees

J IM ALLEGES I FELL IN LOVE WITH HIM THE FIRST TIME HE SERVED *me a steak dinner, and he credits Daytonian Dave Wyse for a major role in our union. Dave coached Jim to blend garlic, soy and Worcestershire to bring out the best in a New York strip. Now on Friday nights when we take the steaks off the grill, we raise a toast in memory of our friend.*

Dave's Grilled New York Strips

2 New York strips (or ribeyes) cut $1\frac{1}{4}$-inches
   thick
Seasoned salt, such as Lawry's
Garlic powder
$\frac{1}{4}$ cup soy sauce
$\frac{1}{4}$ cup Worcestershire sauce

Place steaks on a large platter or baking dish. Lightly dust first side with seasoned salt and garlic powder. Pour half the Worcestershire and soy sauce evenly over the meat. Turn the meat over and repeat the process. Let meat sit in the marinade about 30 minutes; then grill it on direct heat on a preheated gas or charcoal grill. Cook six to eight minutes per side for medium steaks, less for medium rare. Cut with a sharp knife to check for appropriate doneness. Adjust time according to the heat intensity of your grill and thickness of the steak. Serves two to four, depending on who's eating the steak.

J IM IS MASTERFUL AT COOKING STEAKS ON THE TOP OF THE STOVE. *This is a good dish for a day too rainy to use the outdoor grill. We*

prefer the steak seasoned with only salt and pepper, but you can add any seasoning that you like.

Jim's Pan-fried Steak

1 pound sirloin or ribeye, cut $1\frac{1}{4}$-inches thick
Salt, pepper
Seasonings of your choice

Trim fat from steaks and render it in a skillet on high heat. Sprinkle salt and pepper on both sides of the steak. Remove bits of fried fat from the skillet and place steaks in the remaining grease. Sear on high heat for one minute on each side. Lower heat to medium and cook uncovered about five minutes. Turn and cook another five minutes. Check for desired doneness by cutting with a knife. Serves two or three.

ONE DRAWER IN OUR KITCHEN IS DESIGNATED FOR THERMOMETERS: *old-fashioned meat thermometers, instant-read thermometers, deep-fry thermometers, disposable thermometers, oversized forks and spatulas with built-in thermometers. You get the idea. Jim likes to know the temperature of the meat he is cooking. He tries every new thermometer that hits the market, but he trusts his formula more than all these devices. He recommends you cook steak about five or six minutes per side for a 1 $\frac{1}{4}$-inch thickness. Then cut with a knife to see if it's done to your liking.*

Jim's Grilled Steak with Rosemary

New York strip, ribeye or filet, cut $1\frac{1}{4}$-inches
thick (Allow about one-half pound
per person)
Salt, pepper to taste

Garlic powder to taste
Fresh rosemary, finely chopped, to taste

Sprinkle each side of steak with salt, pepper and garlic powder and rub in the rosemary. Grill on direct heat about six minutes per side. Adjust time for thickness. Then cut with a knife to determine if it is cooked to your satisfaction.

WHEN WE MOVED TO GEORGIA, OUR FIRST PLANTING WAS THREE *little sprigs of rosemary. They have thrived and year round we have an abundant supply. Rosemary and lamb are a good combination. If you can't find thick-cut chops, reduce grilling time significantly.*

Jim's Rosemary Lamb Chops

4 lamb chops, cut 1 ½-inches thick
Salt, pepper to taste
Garlic powder to taste
Fresh rosemary, finely chopped, to taste

Sprinkle both sides of chops with salt, pepper and garlic powder. Rub in the rosemary. Grill on direct heat approximately six minutes per side. Cut with a knife to determine if it is cooked to your taste. Serve with a dollop of mint jelly, and accompany the meal with baked sweet potatoes and sautéed spinach.

FRIDAY NIGHT WAS CASUAL MEALTIME AT THE SCHILLO HOUSE ON *Grand Avenue. It was the only day our family had sandwiches for dinner. They were always the same sandwiches — fried steak prepared by my father. Side dishes were tossed salad and thick-cut, homemade French fries.*

Daddy's Steak Sandwiches

1 ½ pounds round steak, cut about ½ inch
    thick
Salt, pepper
Sandwich buns

Trim fat from steak and cut fat into small pieces.
Pound the round steak with a tenderizer or the back
of a heavy kitchen knife. Cut into bun-size pieces.
Fry the fat in a skillet over high heat. Remove solid
pieces and discard (I must admit that as a kid I ate
these fried tidbits). Salt and pepper each piece
of meat and fry in hot grease until well browned
on each side. Serve on a bun with a slice of sweet
onion, pickle and mayonnaise. Makes five or six
sandwiches.

"GOULASH" DEFIES DEFINITION. THE DISH MY MOTHER CALLED
*"goulash" was round steak simmered in tomatoes and green
peppers. The side dishes never varied; goulash was served with a
baked potato, which we sliced in half, mashed a bit and covered with
the vegetables and juices. The salad was a bed of lettuce with two
rings of canned pineapple topped with cottage cheese garnished with
paprika.*

Mother's Goulash

2 ½ pounds round steak
1 can (28 ounces) tomatoes, chopped
Salt, pepper to taste
¼ teaspoon garlic powder
3 large green bell peppers, sliced in strips
2 large onions, sliced in rings

Trim the fat from the steak and cut meat into serving-size pieces. Render the fat in a skillet on high heat. Remove the bits of fat and brown the steak on both sides in the hot drippings. Turn the heat to medium and add tomatoes, salt, pepper, garlic powder, peppers and onions. Bring to a boil. Cover. Reduce temperature to low and simmer about 40 minutes, until meat is tender. About six servings.

WHILE ROUND STEAK WAS A COMMON INGREDIENT IN THE *kitchen of my childhood, spinach was not. Daddy bought it only when he made sukiyaki. He taught me to pronounce the word and to spell it, but until recently I didn't know the derivation. According to one of my international cookbooks, "suki" means hoe, and it is believed that Japanese farmers cooked this dish on their hoes. I prefer preparing it in a big skillet or wok.*

Daddy's Sukiyaki

1 pound round steak
1 tablespoon vegetable oil or cooking spray
$\frac{1}{2}$ pound fresh mushrooms, sliced
1 bunch green onions, cut diagonally in 1-inch
    pieces
3 ribs celery, cut diagonally into 3/4-inch pieces
1 can (5 ounces) sliced bamboo shoots
1 tablespoon soy sauce
1 can (10$\frac{1}{2}$ ounces) condensed beef broth
4 cups fresh spinach, stems removed
2 cups cooked rice

Pound the round steak, remove and discard the fat and cut the meat into strips about two inches long and a half-inch wide. Heat oil in skillet, add meat and brown it on all sides. Push meat to one area of the skillet. Add mushrooms in another area of the pan and the onions, celery and bamboo shoots in the remaining space. Add soy sauce and beef broth and simmer uncovered until vegetables are tender, eight to 10 minutes. Add spinach and simmer another five minutes. Serve over hot rice. Four servings.

WHEN MOTHER SAID, "WE ARE HAVING 'STUFFED MANGOES' FOR *dinner," I knew she was cooking green bell peppers with meat inside. She was not serving the sweet yellow mangoes grown in the tropics. Only in the Midwest have I heard green peppers referred to as "mangoes." A word about Parmesan cheese, too: our family called it "Parmesian," and, oddly enough, so did Jim's family.*

Mother's Stuffed "Mangoes" (Green Peppers)

6 large green bell peppers
2 pounds ground beef
½ cup chopped onion
1 teaspoon salt
¼ teaspoon pepper
1 cup cooked rice
1 can (15 ounces) chopped tomatoes
1 can (8 ounces) tomato sauce
2 tablespoons grated Parmesan cheese

Bring a large pot of water to a boil. Slice tops off the peppers and remove the membrane and seeds. With tongs, lower peppers and tops into the water and simmer four minutes.

Remove peppers and place in a large deep casserole. In a large bowl, mix beef, onion, salt, pepper, rice and chopped tomatoes. Spoon mixture into peppers and place top on each pepper. Sprinkle the grated cheese in the hole of the pepper ring. Pour tomato sauce over peppers. (If you have leftover meat mixture, place it around the peppers.) Bake at 350 degrees about 45 minutes. Six servings.

ON DECEMBER 11, 1940, 23-YEAR-OLD DOROTHA NEWPORT SCHILLO *had a craving for cabbage rolls. Grandma obligingly prepared them for her, and the next day I arrived. You can call me the original "cabbage patch baby."*

Grandma's Cabbage Rolls

2 large heads cabbage
2 pounds ground beef
1 pound ground pork
1 $\frac{1}{2}$ teaspoons salt
$\frac{1}{2}$ teaspoon pepper
$\frac{1}{4}$ teaspoon garlic powder
1 egg, slightly beaten
1 cup cooked rice
1 medium onion, finely diced
1 $\frac{1}{2}$ pounds sauerkraut
1 can (28 ounces) tomatoes, diced

Strip the blemished outer leaves from cabbages and remove most of the cores. Heat a large pot of water to boiling. Carefully lift one head of cabbage into the water and continue boiling until leaves soften and you can remove eight outer leaves with tongs. Repeat the process with the second head of cabbage. Drain the leaves. Refrigerate remaining cabbage for use in another dish.

In a large bowl, combine beef, pork, salt, pepper and garlic powder. Mix in the egg, rice and onion. Shape meat mixture into balls a little smaller than tennis balls. Place each in the center of a cabbage leaf and draw up the sides and secure with a wooden toothpick. (Don't use the colored ones; the dye will stain the cabbage.)

Place each roll, seam side down, in a large, lightly greased baking pan or casserole. When you have used all the meat and leaves, cover the rolls with sauerkraut and pour tomatoes over the sauerkraut. Cover with foil and bake at 375 degrees about 1 $\frac{1}{2}$ hours. Makes about 16 rolls.

IN THE 1950S WHEN I WAS AN ADOLESCENT, THIS DISH WAS MY *birthday entrée. In the past, veal was more economical to purchase than it is now. The recipe requires a rump roast with a bone, rather than the boneless roasts commonly stocked by grocers. Granted, this is a time-consuming recipe.*

Grandma's Veal and Au Gratin Noodles

$\frac{1}{4}$ cup shortening, such as Crisco
4- to 5-pound veal rump roast with bone
Salt, pepper
1 teaspoon garlic powder

Melt the shortening in a roasting pan and brown the meat on high heat. Season with salt, pepper and garlic powder. Place in a 325-degree oven about 2 $\frac{1}{2}$ -3 hours or until thermometer registers 170 degrees. Meanwhile, make the noodles and crumbs and set them aside.

Noodles
8 eggs
About 4 cups flour

Place flour in a mound on a pastry board or in a large bowl. Make a well in the center and add the eggs. Mix with hands or a fork until a ball forms. If necessary, add small amounts of flour. Divide the dough into four parts and with a lightly floured rolling pin on a floured surface, roll the dough about $\frac{1}{4}$-inch thick. Cut with a sharp floured knife or pizza cutter into strips about $\frac{1}{4}$-inch wide and 3 inches long. Lay the noodles flat on a clean tea towel and cover with another. Allow to dry while meat is roasting.

Crumbs
6 slices bread
$\frac{1}{2}$ pound butter (for use in Final Steps)

Toast the bread until it is very dark and dry. Then grate into fine crumbs, using a box grater or blender. Set aside.

Gravy
Pan drippings plus additional shortening,
    if needed, to make 3 tablespoons
3 tablespoons flour
About 2 cups water
Salt, pepper

When meat is done, remove it to a platter and set aside. With a spoon or spatula, scrape the dark bits from the bottom of the pan. Add shortening as needed to make about three tablespoons of drippings. Add flour to the drippings and heat until flour mixture browns, stirring constantly. Add water slowly, a fourth cup at a time, stirring until thickened. Season to taste.

Cut the meat into thick slices and return to the pan with the gravy. Place on warm heat until you have boiled the noodles.

Final Steps

Place noodles in a big pot of boiling water. Cook until they are tender, about 12 minutes. Meanwhile, melt the ½ pound of butter in a large skillet and add the toasted bread crumbs. Heat until well mixed. When noodles are tender, drain them and add to the buttered bread crumbs. Heat until warm.

Serve gravy over both meat and noodles. About eight servings.

THE AROMA OF CHARRED ONIONS WILL PERMEATE THE WHOLE HOUSE *when you make this dish. Use an old pan and be sure to have plenty of Brillo on hand to clean it afterward. When I prepared this entrée for Jim, he was prepared not to like it. He loved it. Serve mashed potatoes on the side and ladle onions and broth over the potatoes.*

Mother's Blackened Onion Pot Roast

2 tablespoons vegetable oil
3 large onions, sliced in rings
2½ to 3-pound chuck roast
Additional 2 tablespoons vegetable oil
1 teaspoon salt
½ teaspoon pepper
Water

In a large deep pan, such as a Dutch oven, heat oil

until almost smoking and put meat inside. Brown quickly on both sides and remove meat from pan. Add additional vegetable oil and heat again on high. Add onions to pot and stir frequently until they are shriveled and blackened.

Return meat to pot and add water to cover. Add salt and pepper and bring to boiling. Cover. Reduce heat and simmer about an hour and a half, until meat is tender. Six servings.

JIM'S BROTHER IS HARDLY AN ICON OF DOMESTICITY. BUT WHEN HE *plays chef aboard* Kinship, *this meal is, as they say, "to die for." He puts the ingredients in a crockpot and it cooks as we cruise all day.*

Jack's Horseradish Pot Roast

Boneless chuck roast (one that will fit into your
   crockpot)
Carrots, pared and cut into chunks
Potatoes, peeled and cut into chunks
Celery, cut into 3-inch pieces
Large onion, sliced
1 jar (6 or 8 ounces) horseradish
$\frac{1}{2}$ cup water
Salt, pepper

Layer vegetables in a crockpot, adding salt and pepper to taste. Place chuck roast on top of the vegetables; season with salt and pepper. Then slather the horseradish on top. Add $\frac{1}{2}$ cup water. Cover and cook on low about seven or eight hours, until meat and vegetables are tender. Four to six servings, depending on size of roast.

As a young bride married to John Thomas in 1964, I had a *short inventory of menus and a tight budget. This was the dish I served our first dinner guests. I modified the original recipe which was in an old Campbell's soup book.*

Company Stroganoff

¼ cup flour
¼ teaspoon salt
¼ teaspoon pepper
¼ cup butter or margarine
1½ pounds round steak, cut into thin strips
1 cup fresh mushrooms, sliced
½ cup chopped onions
1 clove garlic, minced
1 can (10½ ounces) condensed beef broth
1 cup sour cream
4 cups cooked noodles
Paprika

In a gallon-size plastic bag, combine flour, salt and pepper. Add strips of meat and shake. Melt butter in a skillet, add floured meat and brown lightly on all sides. Add mushrooms, onion and garlic and sauté until onions begin to soften. Stir in breef broth and cover. Simmer about an hour, until meat is tender. Blend in sour cream and simmer another five minutes. Serve over hot noodles. Dust with paprika. Four servings.

You could count on prime rib for Christmas dinner when *Jim and Beverly were raising Jason, Matt and Kippy. We continue the tradition, using Bev's recipe. The first time Jim prepared it, he*

forgot to lower the temperature after searing the roast. It turned out fine, but we ate dinner earlier than planned.

Bev's Prime Rib Roast

Standing rib roast (allow one rib per guest or
    more if you want leftovers)
Salt and pepper

Preheat the oven to 450 degrees. Place the meat in a roasting pan and season it generously with salt and pepper. Place the meat in the oven and sear at 450 degrees for five minutes per pound. (For a roast over eight pounds, reduce the searing time by half.) Then lower the oven temperature to 350 degrees. Roast meat until thermometer registers rare (about 15 minutes per pound). Meat will continue cooking when removed from the oven. Let stand 10 minutes before carving.

N O RESTAURANT SERVES MEATLOAF THAT IS COMPARABLE TO PENNY *Darcy's. Our former sister-in-law bakes the meat in loaf pans with racks that are especially designed for meatloaf. This recipe makes two loaves, one for dinner and one for sandwiches or the freezer.*

Penny's Meatloaf

Vegetable oil or cooking spray
$\frac{1}{2}$ cup chopped green pepper
$\frac{1}{2}$ cup chopped onion
1 garlic clove, minced
3 tablespoons brown sugar
$1\frac{1}{3}$ cups catsup
1 tablespoon dry mustard
3 pounds ground beef or combination of beef
    and ground turkey

2 eggs, beaten
Salt, pepper
About ¾ cup breadcrumbs

Heat small amount of vegetable oil in a skillet or spray the pan. Saute green pepper, onion and garlic about five minutes. In a small bowl, mix brown sugar, catsup and dry mustard. Reserve a small amount of the mixture to spread on top of loaves.

Place meat in a large bowl and add sautéed mixture, eggs, and salt and pepper. Add most of the brown sugar mixture and mix well. Add enough breadcrumbs to hold meat together. Shape into two loaves. Spread reserved brown sugar mixture on top of loaves. Place in loaf pans or baking dishes and bake uncovered at 350 degrees for one to one and one-half hours. Four to six servings in each loaf.

EVERY GOOD JEWISH COOK HAS A FAVORITE METHOD FOR MAKING *brisket. Penny's recipe is as good as it gets. For menu nirvana, serve Penny's Noodle Kugel and Grandma's Sweet-Sour Cole Slaw as sides. Make the brisket a day before you plan to serve it.*

Penny's Brisket in Beer

One large onion, chopped
One brisket of beef, well trimmed (allow one-
    half pound per person)
Garlic salt
Salt and pepper
2 cups catsup or more
Bottle of beer
3 tablespoons flour
1 to 2 cups water

Place chopped onions in metal baking pan. Place brisket on top of onions and sprinkle generously with garlic salt and lightly with salt and pepper. "Schmeer" a lot of catsup on it. Pour beer around the meat and cover the pan with foil. Bake at 375 degrees about two hours.

Remove meat from pan and carve into thin slices. Set aside. Place the pan over medium heat (make sure pan is the proper type to put on a stove burner) and add flour to the drippings and onions. Stir and brown; then slowly add water to make desired gravy consistency. Return sliced meat to gravy in pan, cover with foil and return to oven. Bake about another hour, until meat is tender. Remove from oven and chill overnight. The next day, reheat in a low oven before serving.

JIM AND I HAD NOT COOKED FLANK STEAK IN YEARS UNTIL MIKE *Craig reintroduced it to us at his Lake Michigan home, where we dined, viewing the lake and listening to the water lapping the shores. This steak is a lean and tasty cut, but must be marinated at least two hours. You can add various seasonings, if you wish, but this simple preparation is delicious.*

Mike's Grilled Flank Steak

1 ½ to 2-pound flank steak
Soy sauce

Place flank steak in a baking dish and cover generously with soy sauce. Cover with plastic wrap and marinate in the refrigerator two hours or longer. Grill over direct heat about four minutes per side. To serve, cut thin slices across the grain of the meat.

Good with horseradish cream sauce: Mix one to two tablespoons of horseradish with one-half cup sour cream. Four to six servings.

THE RED ROOM IN JIM AND MARY EMERY'S DUBLIN, OHIO, HOME *has a wall-sized screen, a sound system that reverberates in your chest and thousands of films, reflecting the couple's passion for the movies. We are passionate about the meals Mary prepares when we visit. Our favorite dish is bulgogi, the national dish of her native country, Korea.*

Mary's Korean Bulgogi

1 ½ pounds eye of round or similar cut of beef
6 green onions, chopped
1 to 2 cloves garlic, sliced very thin
¾ cup soy sauce
1 ½ tablespoons sesame seeds
2 tablespoons vegetable oil
2 to 3 tablespoons sugar

Slice beef very thin – thinner than a slice of bologna. This is easier if you freeze the meat and partially thaw it before slicing. Pound the slices with the dull side of a large knife to tenderize the meat. In a large bowl, mix the chopped onions and garlic with soy sauce, sesame seeds, oil and sugar. Add the beef and mix. Marinate about an hour in the refrigerator. With a fork or tongs, take meat from bowl and place on a broiler pan and broil two or three minutes. Serve with rice and kimchee if you want to be authentic. Kimchee is pickled cabbage, which you can buy in ethnic markets. You might prefer coleslaw. Four servings.

WHEN GREG AND JENNI'S AUNT CAROLYN THOMAS WAS A *young nurse, she saved her money until she had accumulated an amount sufficient to vacation in Greece for a month. When her funds were depleted, she wasn't ready to come home so she got a job teaching English at the American Farm School and didn't return for a year. When she did come home, she introduced us to "moussaka." It's like a Greek lasagna. If you don't like lamb, you can use all beef in this recipe.*

Carolyn's Moussaka

Bechamel Sauce (make this first)
4 tablespoons butter
2 tablespoons flour
3 cups milk, warmed
Salt and pepper
Nutmeg

Melt butter in a skillet and add flour gradually, stirring constantly with a whisk. Add milk, a little at a time, stirring constantly to avoid lumps. Mixture should be smooth and creamy. Add salt and pepper plus a dash of nutmeg to taste. Set aside.

Moussaka
3 to 4 pounds eggplant
Olive oil
4 tablespoons butter
1 pound ground beef
1 pound ground lamb
2 tablespoons grated onion
2 ripe tomatoes, chopped (or one cup of canned
    chopped tomatoes)
1 tablespoon chopped fresh parsley
$\frac{1}{4}$ teaspoon cinnamon
$\frac{1}{2}$ cup dry red wine (optional)
4 tablespoons grated Parmesan cheese

$\frac{1}{4}$ teaspoon nutmeg
3 eggs, beaten
$\frac{1}{2}$ teaspoon salt
$\frac{1}{4}$ teaspoon pepper
3 cups Béchamel sauce

Rinse the eggplant and cut off ends. Cut crosswise into $\frac{1}{2}$-inch-thick slices. Do not pare the eggplant. Sprinkle slices with salt and let pieces drain in a colander about half an hour to reduce the bitterness. Rinse and pat dry with a paper towel. Brush each slice lightly with olive oil and broil a few minutes until softened and lightly browned.

Melt the butter in a skillet and brown the meat and onions. Add the tomatoes, parsley, cinnamon and wine. Simmer 20 minutes, remove from heat and stir in two tablespoons Bechamel sauce.

Grease a 9x13x2-inch baking dish and place a layer of eggplant in it. Spoon a layer of the meat mixture on top and sprinkle with a portion of the Parmesan cheese. Repeat, ending with eggplant and reserving some cheese. Sprinkle nutmeg on top layer.

In a bowl, mix beaten eggs, salt and pepper into the remaining Bechamel sauce. Pour this mixture over the layers in the baking dish and sprinkle with the remaining Parmesan cheese. Bake at 375 degrees for 40 to 45 minutes, or until top is golden brown. About eight servings.

F OR 30 YEARS, LAKE ERIE WAS JIM'S SANCTUARY FROM THE STRESSES *of caring for cancer patients in Dayton and Columbus. He and his fishing comrades packed the boat with lunches of Spam sandwiches*

and Little Debbies and ample supplies of Erie Dearies and worms to lure the walleyes. At dusk, they lugged their heavy cooler to shore and allowed other fishermen to admire their catch before cleaning the fish and cooking them for dinner. While Jim contends that he hooked me with a fine steak, it might have been the walleye. No professional chef prepares it better. He says it is essential to use a deep-fat thermometer for frying fish.

Jim's Lake Erie Walleye

About 3 pounds walleye fillets
2 eggs
2 cans (4 ounces each) evaporated milk
1 cup breading (purchase prepared breading
    or combine equal parts of flour and
    cornflake crumbs in a plastic bag)
Vegetable oil
1 large sweet onion (optional)

Clean the fish. Remove all bones and soak the fillets in ice cold water five to 10 minutes. Pat dry with a paper towel.

Slightly beat eggs and combine with evaporated milk in a medium-sized bowl. Dip each fillet in the egg mixture; then place in plastic bag with the breading. Shake to coat well. Be prepared to cook the fish soon after breading it.

Pour oil in a heavy deep pan so it's about three inches deep. Heat to 400 degrees. Carefully lower fillets into pan and deep fry three minutes or longer, depending on the thickness of the fillet. Fish should be opaque and flake easily. Serve with thin slices of sweet onion. About six servings.

ONE BIG WALLEYE CAN MAKE A GOOD MEAL FOR FOUR PEOPLE, BUT *it takes a lot of perch to fill a plate. The patience required to catch enough for a meal is rewarded with the first taste of the crisp fillets. These are great piled on a sandwich bun and topped with tartar sauce.*

Jim's Lake Erie Perch

Follow the directions for frying walleye, but cook a shorter time – one to two minutes. Test for flakiness at about a minute and a half.

Tartar Sauce
$\frac{1}{2}$ cup mayonnaise
$1\frac{1}{2}$ tablespoons minced onion
1 tablespoon sweet pickle relish

Combine the ingredients and chill at least one hour before serving. About four servings.

JIM LIKENS CATCHING HALIBUT TO REELING IN A BARN DOOR FROM *the floor of the Pacific Ocean. Muscular son-in-law Andy King understood Jim's comparison when he struggled to land his first halibut in Alaska. He hooked it within minutes of dropping his line to about 300 feet. Several of us stood by cheering. Jim did the cooking.*

Jim's Horseradish Halibut

2 pounds halibut fillets, about 1-inch thick (or cod or grouper)
$\frac{1}{2}$ cup sour cream
$\frac{1}{2}$ cup mayonnaise
2 tablespoons horseradish
$\frac{1}{4}$ teaspoon garlic powder
3 tablespoons soy sauce

$\frac{1}{3}$ cup Italian breadcrumbs
2 tablespoons vegetable oil
1 tablespoon butter or margarine

Preheat oven to 500 degrees. In a bowl, combine sour cream, mayonnaise and horseradish. Run cold water over fish and pat dry. Place fillets on a large dish. Sprinkle them with garlic powder and douse them with soy sauce. Slather sour cream mixture on the fillets and sprinkle breadcrumbs on top.

Heat a baking pan in the hot oven about 5 minutes. Remove and put oil and margarine in the hot pan, moving it about until the bottom is coated. Transfer fish into baking pan and bake at 500 degrees about 18 minutes or until the fish flakes easily with a fork. Cooking time depends on thickness of the fish; the topping insulates the fish so it may take longer. Test the fish at 12 minutes. About six servings.

WE DO NOT FISH FOR CHILEAN SEA BASS (ALSO KNOWN AS *toothfish*), *but we buy it at the market when it's not on the endangered list and not exorbitantly expensive. This recipe can be used with any mild fish, including grouper and snapper. It is best cut an inch thick.*

Jim's Baked Chilean Sea Bass

1 egg
1 can (4 ounces) evaporated milk
2 pounds fish fillets, cut one-inch thick
$\frac{1}{3}$ cup Italian breadcrumbs
$\frac{1}{3}$ cup shredded Parmesan cheese
$\frac{1}{3}$ cup shredded mozzarella cheese
2 tablespoons butter or margarine

Preheat oven to 500 degrees. In a medium-sized bowl, mix the egg and milk. Place fillets in the mixture. In a separate bowl, mix breadcrumbs, Parmesan and mozzarella. Remove fish from the egg mixture and dip fillets in the breading, coating them well.

Heat a baking pan in the oven a couple of minutes. Remove the heated pan and place butter in it, moving it to coat the bottom. Place breaded fillets in the hot pan, return it to the oven and bake approximately 15 minutes, until the fish is opaque and flakes easily. Six servings.

SINCE CAPTAIN JACK LAUNCHED THE ORIGINAL KINSHIP IN 1995, HE *has spent most summers in Alaska where salmon is the catch of choice. This simple recipe is the one we most commonly use aboard.*

Captain Jack's Grilled Salmon

2 pounds salmon fillets, one-inch thick
1 cup bottled Italian salad dressing, such as
    Paul Newman's

Lay fish fillets in a baking dish and pour Italian dressing over them. Marinate one-half to one hour. Grill on direct heat about five minutes per side or until fish flakes easily. Six servings.

SON-IN-LAW NED DISPLAYED HIS CULINARY EXPERTISE WHEN HE *prepared this savory salmon dish. He offers no measurements; he suggests you suit your own taste in the amounts of spices and herbs to use. His friend, a Cleveland jeweler nicknamed "Mooshie," is his recipe source.*

Ned and Mooshie's Broiled Salmon

1 large salmon fillet (allow ⅓ pound per
    person)
Garlic powder or fresh cloves of garlic, minced
Salt
Ground ginger
Dried dill weed
Mayonnaise
Parmesan cheese, grated

Sprinkle garlic, salt, ginger and dill weed on fish.
"Schmeer" on some mayonnaise, but not too heavily.
Sprinkle with Parmesan. Place on broiler pan and
broil until fish flakes. Cooking time will depend on
thickness of fillet. Check a one-inch fillet at eight
minutes. It might take as long as 12 minutes.

B E FOREWARNED: WHEN YOU SPEND A NIGHT AT OUR HOME, YOU *may be put to work. My Colonel White High School friend and Ohio University sorority sister, Sue Jones Pease, and her husband Ed were unsuspecting guests when they visited us in Georgia. They seemed pleased when Jim said he would serve fish for dinner. Sue remarked that she had a speedy way to prepare tilapia. You guessed it: Jim bought tilapia and Sue prepared our entrée. We've used her stovetop method with other mild fish with equal success.*

Sue's Sauteed Tilapia

2 tablespoons butter
4 tilapia fillets
Garlic salt
Pepper
Dried oregano
Paprika

Heat butter in a skillet. Dust fish with garlic salt, pepper, oregano and paprika. Saute about two minutes on each side. Good served with fried potatoes and steamed spinach. Serves four.

IN MY CHILDHOOD, WE ATE CATFISH DREDGED IN A CORNMEAL-*flour mix and fried in fat. The heavy coating helped mask the strong flavor. Now the catfish you buy in the grocery is farm-raised and mild. Jim found an appealing recipe on a package of catfish and fine-tuned it to his liking.*

Jim's Catfish in Orange Sauce

1 tablespoon vegetable oil
2 tablespoons green onions, sliced
1 teaspoon chopped fresh rosemary
$\frac{1}{3}$ cup orange juice
Grated zest from one orange
Dash pepper
$\frac{1}{2}$ teaspoon salt
1 pound catfish fillets
Parsley (optional)
Orange slices (optional)

Heat the oil in a large skillet over medium heat. Add onions and cook until softened, but not browned. Add rosemary, orange juice, zest, pepper and salt. Stir and cook one minute. Add fillets and reduce heat to medium low. Cover and cook eight to 10 minutes, or until fish flakes easily. Place fillets on serving dish and spoon sauce over them. Garnish with parsley and orange slices. Three servings.

Trolley Stop

THE YELLOW ELECTRIC TROLLEY BUS ROLLED THROUGH THE STREETS *of Dayton, so crowded that some people had to stand, swaying and hanging onto a bar above their heads to keep their balance. To alert the driver to let them off, passengers pulled a black cord that stretched the length of the bus over the windows. When I was a little girl riding downtown with Mother, she held me by the waist while I stood on the seat to reach the mechanism.*

But when Mother and I rode the bus to Grandma and Grandpa Newport's house, we had no need to signal the driver. We usually were the only ones left at the last stop beyond the west borders of Dayton. The bus made its wide turn in a lot right next to my maternal grandparents' house that Grandpa and Uncle Denny built out of gray cinder blocks. After they constructed it, they soon added another room, a gigantic one on the front of the building. I suppose Grandma envisioned it would be a grand living room, but it was big enough to turn into a restaurant, and that's what my uncle did with it. He turned it into an eatery and called it Denny's Restaurant.

I WISH I COULD TELL YOU THAT IT WAS THE ORIGIN OF THE DENNY'S *Restaurants that you see today, but it wasn't. My entrepreneurial uncle – who lived his entire adult life in the house behind the restaurant with his parents – tried his hand at numerous businesses. None made him wealthy. After he started the restaurant, he built a garage for repairing cars at the rear of the property, and on the lot east of the house, he opened a furniture store. Occasionally, I peeked into the garage where the auto mechanics raised their heads from beneath propped-up hoods and waved their greasy hands to greet me.*

I was fascinated with all of Uncle Denny's enterprises, but it was the restaurant I loved the most. When I got to be nine or 10, he let me approach the red vinyl booths with a little green-lined pad of paper in hand to take orders from customers. Then I'd run behind the counter to tell my uncle what they wanted. I thought he made the best hamburgers and grilled cheese sandwiches in the world. I got the patrons' drinks myself, reaching into a massive red metal cooler filled with ice and lifting out dripping bottles of Coke and orange drink. I preferred grape Nehi myself. I liked the color, the taste and the shape of the bottle, and my uncle let me drink as many as I wanted — for free. He also gave me an unlimited supply of nickels to drop in the slot of the colorful jukebox. And, when nobody else was around, he gave me handfuls of metal slugs to play the pinball machines.

My uncle was the only one in our entire family who traveled, and he brought back exotic toys for me, including an Indian head carved from a coconut from Florida and hand-painted castanets from Mexico. Once he bought a brand-new red Ford convertible and drove it directly to our house so I could be the first person to ride in it with the top down.

WHEN I WAS OLD ENOUGH, MY ENTERPRISING UNCLE LET ME HELP IN HIS RESTAURANT

BUT, I DIGRESS. IT'S MY GRANDMA NEWPORT'S cooking that I wanted to tell you about. I remember her making Mother and me hot peppermint tea when we arrived on a cold day. Some days, it was sassafras. I liked that too; it tasted like hot root beer. When we walked in the door, we always smelled dinner cooking on the old gas stove. Grandma usually had a fat hen stewing in rich yellow broth. She'd let me cut the "pot pie" she had rolled out, and then she would slide the squares of dough into the hot broth.

Before Mother and I left, Grandma led me to the chicken coop behind the house. She supervised as I tentatively slipped my hand under the warm bodies of the banty hens *to extract the small brown eggs she would send home with us. Then Grandma stood at the door waving to us as we boarded the yellow city bus for our ride back to Grand Avenue.*

The old decaying buildings were dismantled after Grandpa and Grandma and Uncle Denny died, and I have no idea if the bus still turns in the circle. I must check it out the next time I go to Dayton. I'd like to ride it one more time.

Grandma Newport's Chicken and Pot Pie

1 whole stewing or roasting chicken, cut into pieces
    (remove and discard the neck and organ parts)
½ cup chopped celery
½ cup chopped onion
1 teaspoon salt
½ teaspoon pepper

Place pieces of chicken in a large pot; cover with water and bring to a boil. Remove the scum that surfaces. Add celery, onion, salt and pepper and simmer, partially covered, one hour, or until chicken is tender. Meanwhile, prepare the pot pie.

Pot Pie
1 ¼ cups flour
¼ teaspoon baking soda
½ teaspoon salt
⅓ cup shortening, such as Crisco (I think Grandma used lard.)
About 3 tablespoons water

Sift flour, baking soda and salt together in a medium bowl. Cut in shortening and add water a tablespoon at a time until pastry sticks together and can be formed into a ball. On floured surface, roll out about ¼-inch thick and cut into 2-inch squares.

When the chicken is tender, remove the pieces, increase heat and slide squares of pastry into the boiling broth. Lower heat and simmer 15 minutes, uncovered. Then return chicken to pot to reheat. Four to six servings, depending on size of chicken.

AWARD-WINNING DAYTON WRITER, ANITA RICHWINE, WHO HAILS *from Arnie Palmer and Mr. Roger's hometown of Latrobe, Pennsylvania, has warm memories of her mother-in-law's Pennsylvania Dutch version of pot pie. Her family called it "bot boi."*

Anita's Mother-in-Law's Beef "Bot Boi'

2 pounds stewing beef, pork or veal, cut into
    1-inch pieces
Salt, pepper

Place meat in a large pot and cover with water. Add salt and pepper and simmer for $1\frac{1}{2}$ hours. In the meantime, prepare the dough.

"Bot Boi"
3 tablespoons shortening, such as Crisco
$1\frac{1}{2}$ cups flour
1 teaspoon salt
1 egg, beaten (optional)
A little water or milk (more if egg is omitted)
Saffron (optional)

Cut shortening into flour and salt. Add beaten egg and enough water or milk to form dough. Roll out thin on lightly floured board and cut into 2-inch squares.

Vegetables

6 potatoes, sliced
1 onion, sliced

When meat is tender, slowly drop layers of dough squares, potatoes and onions into the boiled meat and broth. There should be enough liquid to boil up over top of pot pie. Canned beef broth can be used for additional liquid, if needed. Cover tightly and simmer 20 minutes. A pinch of saffron may be added, if desired. Six to eight servings.

Note: For chicken "bot boi," put layers of cut-up chicken, potatoes and onion slices and dough squares into pot of boiling, salted water. Cook slowly until chicken and potatoes are done.

CINDY FOX (WHO JOINED OUR FAMILY VIA HER MARRIAGE TO *"surrogate" son Jay Kyne) is surely the most attentive realtor in all of Raleigh, North Carolina. She "stages" sellers' homes so they are inspection-perfect for potential buyers, and she sponsors an annual fun-filled "pig-pickin' party" for her clients. When buyers move into their new homes, she arrives at their doorstep with this homey pot pie from a recipe passed to her by Myra Nelson, her ex-sister-in-law.*

Cindy and Myra's Chicken Pot Pie

2 refrigerated pie crusts, such as Pillsbury
2 cups cooked chicken, cut into cubes
1 can (15-ounces) mixed vegetables, such as Veg-All
2 cans cream of potato soup (Cindy prefers Campbell's)
½ teaspoon dried, crushed thyme
½ teaspoon black pepper

½ cup milk
1 egg, slightly beaten (optional)

Place one pie crust in pie pan and bake in preheated 450-degree oven about 10 minutes. In a large bowl, mix the cooked chicken, vegetables, potato soup, thyme, pepper and milk. Spoon into the baked pie crust.

Place the unbaked pie crust on top of the mixture and crimp and seal edges. Cut slits in top pie crust. Bake 25 to 30 minutes in 450-degree oven. Remove from oven and brush beaten egg on top. Return to oven and bake another 10 to 15 minutes, until crust is lightly browned. Six servings.

WHEN THEY WERE YOUNGSTERS, JENNI AND GREG SPENT EVERY *other weekend with their father. One day they returned from his home in Columbus raving about a dish he had prepared. They were proud to teach me how to make it.*

John's Chicken in Pastry

4 ounces cream cheese, softened
½ cup sour cream
2 tablespoons butter, melted
2 cups chicken, cooked and cubed
¼ teaspoon garlic powder
¼ teaspoon salt
Dash of pepper
1 tablespoon onion, minced
1 package refrigerated crescent rolls
Additional 2 tablespoons butter, melted
Additional sour cream (optional)
Salsa (optional)

Blend cream cheese, sour cream and melted butter. Add the chicken, seasonings and onion to the mixture. Separate crescent dough into four rectangles. Lay each rectangle on a baking sheet and press out the perforations. Spoon one-fourth of the chicken mixture onto the center of each rectangle and pull up the corners of each piece of dough over the chicken. Pinch seams together and brush with melted butter. Bake at 350 degrees about 20 minutes or until pastry is golden and puffy. Serve with sour cream and salsa. Four servings.

PEOPLE FIND IT HARD TO BELIEVE THAT THIS DISH CAN BE SO EASY *and taste so good. I credit Sandy Oswald — a working mother like me on the marketing staff at St. Elizabeth Medical Center in the 1980s — for passing on this technique.*

Sandy's Crockpot Turkey

1 whole turkey breast (a size that will fit
    into your crockpot)
Salt, pepper
Paprika

Place whole turkey breast in crockpot and sprinkle with salt, pepper and paprika or seasonings of your choice. Cover and heat on low all day (eight or nine hours). Six to eight servings.

WHEN JIM AND JACK CRUISED ON KINSHIP WITH NO CREW, THEY *discovered a few menus items that required basic ingredients and a minimum of effort. This was one of their simple-to-prepare entrees.*

Jack and Jim's Chicken Parmesan

1 jar (about 20 ounces) prepared marinara sauce
    (or pasta sauce of your choice)
4 boneless chicken breasts
⅓ cup shredded mozzarella cheese
⅓ cup grated parmesan
⅓ cup Italian breadcrumbs
2 tablespoons melted butter or margarine

Pour half the sauce in bottom of a medium-sized baking dish. Place chicken over the sauce and pour remaining sauce on top. In a small bowl, mix mozzarella and Parmesan with breadcrumbs and melted butter. Sprinkle over chicken. Bake in preheated 350-degree oven about 35 minutes or until chicken is tender and juices run clear. Four servings.

AFTER GRADUATION FROM OHIO UNIVERSITY'S JOURNALISM SCHOOL *in the early 1960s, Sherry Jessup and I shared an apartment near the shores of the Miami River in Dayton. I was a writer for the* Dayton Journal Herald; *she was director of public relations for the Dayton chapter of the American Red Cross.*

We lived frugally; both of us were tucking away money for our trousseaus. Each week we allocated $10 for groceries, faithfully snipped coupons and shopped together with an eye for meat cuts we could stretch into several meals.

Soon Sherry married Ralph Walls and we went our separate ways. In the mid-1990s, we reunited shortly after she was widowed. She invited Jim and me to come for dinner at her Columbus home. When we arrived, she presented our meal on a little table she had set close to the fireplace. It was a warm and cozy setting for catching up on our years of separation. She served this dish.

Sherry's Chicken Enchiladas

1 pound skinless, boneless chicken breasts
4 cups fresh spinach, torn in small pieces, or
    10 ounces frozen, drained chopped spinach
$\frac{1}{4}$ cup green onions, sliced thin
1 cup sour cream
$\frac{1}{2}$ cup plain fat-free yogurt
3 tablespoons flour
$\frac{1}{2}$ teaspoon cumin
$\frac{1}{4}$ teaspoon salt
$\frac{1}{2}$ cup milk
1 can (4 ounces) diced green chilies, drained
6 7-inch tortillas
$\frac{1}{3}$ cup shredded cheddar cheese
Salsa
Green onions, sliced

Place chicken in a saucepan and cover with water. Bring to a boil; then reduce heat and cover with a lid. Simmer until chicken is white throughout, about 15 minutes. Remove chicken from pan and cool. Then shred into bite-sized pieces. Set aside.

If using fresh spinach, cook it in a steamer over boiling water about four minutes. Drain. If using frozen, prepare as directed on the package and drain. In a large bowl, mix together the shredded chicken, spinach and green onions. Set aside. In a smaller bowl, combine sour cream, yogurt, flour, cumin and salt. Stir in milk and chilies. Divide sauce in half and set aside.

Add half the sauce to the chicken-spinach mixture. Spoon equal portions of the filling into each tortilla and roll up. Place seam side down in a lightly greased 9x13-inch baking dish. Spoon reserved sauce over tortillas and bake uncovered in a 350-degree oven about 25 minutes or until heated throughout. Remove from oven; sprinkle with cheddar. Serve with salsa and green onions. Six servings.

ONE OF GRANDMA'S WINTERTIME STANDARDS WAS A DISH SHE *called Pork and Knodels , which we pronounced ka-NAY-duls. To eat the knodels, or bread dumplings, we cut them in half and spooned the caraway broth over them. Grandma purchased her caraway at the bakery; she feared the packages available at the supermarket were old and lacked flavor.*

Grandma's Pork and Knodels

4-pound Boston butt pork roast
3 tablespoons caraway seeds
12 cups water
1-pound loaf sliced white bread, at least
    a day old
1 large potato
$\frac{1}{2}$ cup flour
$\frac{1}{2}$ teaspoon salt
2 eggs, beaten
Horseradish (optional)

Place pork, caraway and water into a large pot. Bring to a boil and then lower the heat and simmer, partially covered, about $1\frac{1}{2}$ to 2 hours or until tender (an inserted thermometer registers 170 degrees).

In the meantime, break up a loaf of white bread into small pieces. Pare and grate a large potato. Mix the bread pieces and the grated potato in a large bowl. Add flour, eggs and salt. Mix with your hands and shape into six to eight balls about the size of a baseball.

When it is fully cooked, remove the meat from the broth. Bring the broth to boiling and lower each knodel into the pot with a big spoon. Cover partially with a lid and simmer about 20 minutes.

Slice the meat and add it to the pot and reheat it. Serve the meat with knodel halves topped with broth. Serve horseradish on the side. Serves six to eight.

Baked ham is our traditional Easter entrée. I learned to buy *a large ham so there would be plenty left for cold ham sandwiches and for deviled ham sandwiches as well.*

Grandma's Deviled Ham

4 cups leftover cooked ham, cubed
1 cup mayonnaise
¼ cup minced onion
½ cup sweet pickle relish

Grind the ham or swirl it in the food processor until it is the texture of ground beef. In a small bowl, combine mayonnaise, onion and relish. Add to the ground ham. If needed, add some pickle juice or more mayonnaise to make it a spreadable consistency. Makes six to eight sandwiches.

Cooking for 35 people is a challenge for me, but I managed *to successfully feed our extended family at a weeklong reunion held at our home in Georgia. Our Southern buffet welcoming dinner featured pulled pork sandwiches that were a hit with our West Coast and Midwest gang. Not one person, however, appreciated the boiled peanuts I offered. I've scaled this pork recipe for a smaller group.*

Reunion Pulled Pork

4 to 5-pound Boston butt pork roast
1 tablespoon salt
1 teaspoon pepper
2 cloves garlic, minced
Water
3 cups catsup
¾ cup finely chopped onions
3 tablespoons brown sugar
¾ teaspoon ground allspice
⅓ cup vinegar
3 tablespoons Worcestershire
¾ cup water
Sweet pickle slices or slaw (optional)

Rub salt, pepper and garlic into roast and place in a large pot. Cover half way up the meat with water and bring to a boil. Reduce heat and simmer about three hours, partially covered, until meat falls from the bone. Turn the meat over about halfway through the cooking.

In the meantime, place catsup, onions, brown sugar, allspice, vinegar, Worcestershire and water into a medium saucepan and simmer about 30 minutes.

When the meat is tender, drain and cool it. With a fork, shred the cooled meat and place it in a large saucepan. Mix in the barbecue sauce. Reheat about 10 minutes. Serve with sweet pickle slices or slaw on toasted buns. Makes about eight sandwiches.

No Experience Necessary

N O OHIO UNIVERSITY GRADUATE HAD A CLEARER GOAL THAN JOAN *Marie Schillo: I wanted to be a writer for the* Dayton Journal Herald, *which was the morning newspaper. I had interned there two summers and had rubbed shoulders with such stalwart state reporters as Bob Daley, fearless police beat writers as Ann Heller, and diligent editors like Ted Bingham. I intended to be part of their fraternity of journalists.*

My interview for a permanent position went well. "We've watched you and we've worked with you and we want you here," John Moore, the managing editor, informed me.

His words were uplifting, until I heard the hitch. "The only problem," he said hesitantly, watching for my reaction, "is that there is only one job opening, and it's in the women's department."

I could not conceal my disappointment. I did not consider the "women's department," as it was called in the 1960s, a terrain for serious journalists.

"G IVE IT A CHANCE," HE SUGGESTED, WHEN HE RECOGNIZED MY *dismay. "Meet Marj. Maybe you will change your mind."*

Reluctantly, I agreed to meet Marj Heyduck, the "women's editor," who was a celebrity in our city and was highly regarded by professionals throughout the country. But I knew that a position in the newspaper section that featured advice columns, recipes and wedding pictures was not my calling.

After an hour's discussion with Marj, I executed a 180-degree turn in my attitude and accepted her employment proposition. I realized later that my decision to accept the position was the most significant step in my career. Marj was the finest coach a young writer could have. A mentor, a motivator, a friend: she was all of them. Even Erma Bombeck – who became revered throughout the country – sought counsel from Marj.

Y OU WONDER HOW THIS INCIDENT RELATES TO COOKING? WELL, *Marj designated me the food writer. Fresh out of college, I could claim experience only at my mother's elbow. I was intimidated by the assignment.*

"No matter," said Marj. "You don't have to be good at cooking. You have to be good writing about it."

And so I wrote about foods and cooking. I also read about cooking. I studied every new cookbook that was sent to the office for review. And eventually I cooked.

This is a slightly revised recipe from the first cookbook I ever read page by page. It was my primer: Cooking with Soup, *published in the early 1960s by the Campbell Soup Company. The firm, which was founded in 1869 as the Joseph A. Campbell Preserve Company, produced canned vegetables, meats and preserves. In 1897, a chemist, who was paid $7.50 a week, invented condensed soups and revolutionized the industry. In 1916, a cookbook called "Helps for the Hostess" was the first book to offer recipes using condensed soup as an ingredient. Now, according to the Campbell organization, some 440 million cans of condensed soup are used every year in recipes. The Campbell website features hundreds for you to try.*

Fruit-Topped Pork Chops

Cooking spray
4 pork chops
4 slices tart apple, such as Granny Smith, about
    $\frac{1}{2}$-inch thick
4 orange slices, about $\frac{1}{2}$-inch thick
$\frac{1}{4}$ teaspoon cinnamon
Dash of ground cloves
1 can ($10\frac{1}{2}$ ounces) low-salt, condensed beef
    broth
1 tablespoon dark brown sugar
2 tablespoons fresh orange juice
1 tablespoon cornstarch

Grease skillet with cooking spray; brown chops on both sides. Place an apple and an orange slice on each chop. Sprinkle with cinnamon and cloves.

Mix beef broth and sugar and add to the skillet. Cover; simmer about 35 minutes, until meat is white throughout. Remove meat and fruit from the pan. Mix orange juice and cornstarch in a small dish until smooth; gradually blend into the broth. Heat, stirring constantly, until slightly thickened. Return meat and fruit to pan and simmer a few minutes more until heated throughout. Four servings.

As young mothers with preschoolers, Helen Hoke and I *shared cooking discoveries when we were neighbors on Lynnfield Drive in Kettering, Ohio. I've lost touch with her, but I've always held onto – and used – this recipe that she gave me.*

Helen's Hot Ham and Cheese Sandwiches

¼ pound margarine, at room temperature
3 tablespoons mustard (yellow or Dijon)
2 tablespoons poppy seeds
1 teaspoon Worcestershire
1 onion, chopped
1 pound boiled ham, thinly sliced
1 pound Swiss cheese, thinly sliced
8 sandwich buns

Mix the margarine, mustard, poppy seeds, Worcestershire and onion. Spread on both sides of buns. Layer ham and cheese on buns and close. Wrap each sandwich in foil. Bake 20 minutes at 325 degrees. These freeze well. Make the sandwiches and wrap them and place in the freezer. Bake them when you want to serve them; no need to thaw first. Makes eight sandwiches.

IN JULY 2000, GREG AND CARRIE'S KITCHEN WAS STRIPPED OF ITS *cabinets and appliances. The contractor missed his due date, but newborn Scott did not. After his arrival, Carrie tended the baby, I helped entertain Big Sis Erika and Greg did all the cooking for a couple of weeks on the outdoor grill. The pizza he made was quick, easy and delicious.*

Greg's Grilled Pizza

> 1 medium-sized prepared pizza crust, such as
>   Boboli
> 1 cup prepared pizza sauce
> $\frac{1}{2}$ cup pepperoni, sliced
> $\frac{1}{2}$ cup fresh mushrooms, sliced
> $\frac{1}{2}$ cup onions, finely chopped
> 2 cups shredded mozzarella
> Italian seasonings

> Preheat grill to a high temperature. Spread pizza sauce on crust and add toppings, ending with a sprinkling of Italian seasonings. Place crust on grill rack. Cover and cook seven or eight minutes, or until cheese melts. Six to eight pieces.

PESTO, PINE NUTS AND TORTELLINI ARE PERFECT FLAVOR PARTNERS. *Long ago, Barbara Cebuhar, who now lives in Virginia, served them at a dinner party in Dayton. She accompanied the pasta dish with a crisp romaine salad and crusty bread. You can purchase pesto in a jar, but it's easy to make and tastes remarkably fresher.*

Barb's Tortellini and Pesto

> 8 ounces tortellini

⅓ cup pine nuts
⅓ cup pesto
Parmesan for topping

Cook the tortellini according to package directions. Drain and add pine nuts and pesto. Mix thoroughly. Sprinkle with Parmesan. Four servings.

Fresh Pesto
1 cup fresh basil leaves, chopped
3 tablespoons pine nuts
2 cloves garlic
¼ cup grated Parmesan
2 tablespoons olive oil

Place basil, pine nuts, garlic, and Parmesan in a blender. Slowly add oil and blend until smooth.

The Blessings of Blending

JIM AND I FRETTED AS WE PREPARED FOR THE HOLIDAY GATHERING *at our new Worthington, Ohio, home. Technically, our guests were family, but many members of this recently merged group were not well acquainted and some had never met.*

My "bonus" children — the term we prefer to "stepchildren" — and their spouses and Jim's bonus family were looking forward to the get-together. Counting the grandchildren, there were 15 of us in the immediate family at the time.

However, for this occasion, we extended the invitations well beyond immediate family. Among the guests would be my ex-husband John, Jenni and Greg's father. Jim's side of the family had never met him. A bearded, politically liberal and sometimes outspoken fellow with a dry sense of humor, John said he would bring his current girlfriend if that was okay with us. "Sure," we said, "that's fine."

John's second ex-wife, a woman who lived near us and with whom we've stayed in touch, said she would stop by with her son Michael, who is Jenni and Greg's half-brother.

Son Matt told us that he and his wife Melissa would be accompanied by Lanell and Robert, Melissa's parents who were visiting from Louisiana. We had had little contact with them, but were aware of their conservative views and deeply religious background.

Son Jason, active in a Big Brothers organization, planned to bring the "little brother" he was mentoring, a teenager with a troubled past who recently was released from a juvenile facility. I recall Jason saying something about this being a good opportunity for the youngster to observe the functioning of a "normal" family.

JIM AND I WERE EDGY AS GUESTS STARTED ARRIVING. WE DECIDED *to take a chance on playing an ice breaker. As people entered our home, we taped cards on their backs, designating each as a well-known personality. Each person was to guess his or her new identity by asking other guests questions that could be answered by only "yes" or "no."*

With some uncertainty, they began circulating through the house, from kitchen to family room to dining room to the sun room, asking one another questions such as: "Am I alive?" "Am I beautiful?" "Am I someone you'd like to have dinner with?"

As Snow White met Abraham Lincoln and as Jesus Christ chatted with Madonna, the noise level rose and guffaws and belly laughs filled the house. The toddlers, taking cues from the fellowship, willingly accepted hugs and pats from people who moments before were strangers.

Soon we settled around the tables we had pushed together to accommodate the crowd, offered a prayer of thanks and passed the food.

W HY HAD WE WORRIED AT ALL? EVEN IF THE GAME HAD FAILED, *the meal would have united this group. Lanell brought a massive casserole of Southern cornbread stuffing and divulged her "secret ingredient." Daughter Kippy presented her usual mountain of mashed potatoes, and Jim carved the giant gobbler as John poured the wine. The girlfriend, who turned out to be a pleasant addition to the group, passed fresh bread she had baked. Some dug into the succotash while others piled on the green beans. Some snubbed the sweet potatoes; others dipped in for seconds. Everyone held plates up for Greg's traditional pumpkin pies and then for wedges of homemade pecan pie that Jason had laced with bourbon.*

Together, we entertained the grandchildren, listened to Robert's yarns and chuckled at John's jokes. And throughout the meal, we reminisced about the loved ones, who — because of travel distance — could not be with us. Sisters-in-law Betsy and Carolyn were dining with friends in far-off Idaho and Massachusetts. Jim's brother's family, our West Coast contingent, were in California where we could picture Jack slicing the turkey and serving dinner to a disparate flock that bore resemblance to our own.

There we were. To an observer, we would appear the personification of a Rockwell tableau. Yet we were an eclectic bunch of Catholics and Methodists, Baptists and agnostics...sweet potato lovers and sweet potato haters...Yankees and Confederates...couples unloosed by law and "bonus' siblings created by a new union. There we were — breaking bread and witnessing thankfulness for one another.

Vegetables and Other Side Dishes

DURING AN ALASKAN EXPEDITION ON KINSHIP, EIGHT FAMILY *members rotated into the galley for dinner duties. On Kippy and Andy's meal-making night, Kippy announced she would make mashed potatoes, her specialty. I can't remember what she and Andy prepared as the entrée, but I well recall the potatoes. She produced a 10-pound bag and with Andy's assistance, pared and cooked every potato. It was the biggest mass of potatoes ever served from that galley. Of course, in Ungerleider style, we polished off every bite. Here is her recipe cut in half.*

Kippy's Famous Mashed Potatoes

5 pounds potatoes
$\frac{1}{2}$ stick butter
Approximately $\frac{1}{2}$ cup milk
Salt

Boil potatoes until soft. Drain. Mash potatoes by hand with a potato masher. Slice butter and add it to the hot potatoes. Add milk and salt. With an electric mixer, begin mixing. Whip potatoes until they appear light and fluffy. You may need to add additional milk.

With your finger, scoop a taste to determine if more salt needs to be added. Once taste desire is reached, serve potatoes. Kippy would tell you this serves five people. Use your own judgment.

Horseradish Mashed Potatoes

Kippy, purist that she is, disdains any variation; but you might want to try this: add about one or two tablespoons of horseradish to Kippy's mashed potato recipe.

MOTHER NEVER COMPLAINED ABOUT THE TIME IT TOOK TO *grate potatoes for pancakes, but one time I opted to dodge this laborious step by using my food processor. I didn't like the result and won't be tempted to try it again. A hand grater is simply required to duplicate the taste of my mother's pancakes.*

Also, I have learned that cooking spray is not a satisfactory substitute for good old-fashioned Crisco for frying them. While we Schillo's served "potato pancakes," our Jewish neighbors called them "latkes," and they served them during Chanukah. These pancakes should be flat and crispy around the edges. You need to cook the pancakes as soon as you make the batter.

Mother's Potato Pancakes

6 medium potatoes, grated on the large holes of
    a box grater
1 medium onion, grated on the large holes of a
    box grater
2 eggs
1 ½ tablespoons flour
1 teaspoon salt
About ¾ cup shortening, such as Crisco
Sour cream (optional)
Applesauce (optional)

In a large bowl, mix the grated potatoes and grated onion with the eggs. Stir in the flour and salt. Heat the shortening in a skillet. Use enough shortening so it is about ¼-inch deep in the skillet when melted. Spoon about two tablespoons of batter for each pancake into the hot shortening. If the batter doesn't sizzle a bit when you put it into the pan, the shortening isn't hot enough. Fry until lightly brown on each side, about two minutes.

Liquid will keep rising to the top of the batter. Spoon it off and discard it as you make the pancakes. Transfer pancakes to a paper-towel-lined plate and keep warm in a 200-degree oven until you have used all the batter. Serve with sour cream or applesauce. Makes about 20 small pancakes.

I ATE SO MUCH POTATO SALAD AT FAMILY PICNICS WHEN I WAS A CHILD *that I steered away from it in my adult years. However, I savored the potato salad that daughter-in-law Carrie's mother brought to a party celebrating Erika's first holy communion. Rose Ann tells me that her own mother used homemade mayonnaise, but she prefers using slaw dressing.*

Rose Ann's Potato Salad

4 or 5 medium-sized white potatoes, not pared
⅔ cup onions, finely diced
About ⅔ cup slaw dressing (Rose Ann
    uses Marzetti's)
About one teaspoon mustard, enough to
    give slight color
Salt, pepper to taste
3 hard-boiled eggs, chopped
1 hard-boiled egg, sliced

Place potatoes in their skins in a large pot of cold water. Bring to boil and boil 15 to 20 minutes, until a fork pierces them easily. (Take care not to overcook.) Drain the water and rinse the potatoes in cold water. Then remove skins. Cube the potatoes into bite-sized pieces.

Gently combine the potatoes with diced onions. Mix slaw dressing, mustard and salt and pepper and add to potato-onion mixture, using an amount that moistens the potatoes to your satisfaction. Fold in the three chopped eggs. Place in serving dish and smooth the mixture with the back of a spoon. Garnish with remaining sliced eggs. Chill at least two hours. About six servings.

RED AND GREEN BELL PEPPERS MAKE THIS DISH APPEALING FOR THE *Christmas holidays. You can use regular sour cream and cheddar, but our family is content with the lower-fat versions.*

Family-Pleasing Hash Brown Casserole

1 package (32 ounces) frozen hash browns (the
    shredded type, not the cubed potatoes)
1 teaspoon salt
$\frac{1}{4}$ teaspoon pepper
$\frac{1}{2}$ cup onion, chopped
1 can (10$\frac{1}{2}$ ounces) condensed cream of chicken
    soup
2 cups reduced-fat sour cream
$\frac{1}{2}$ green bell pepper, chopped
$\frac{1}{2}$ red bell pepper, chopped
2 cups sharp, low-fat cheddar, shredded
2 cups cornflakes, crushed
$\frac{1}{4}$ cup butter or margarine, melted

In a large bowl, combine frozen potatoes, salt, pepper, onions, soup, sour cream, green and red peppers and cheese. Mix well by hand. Place in a large greased casserole. Mix cornflakes and melted butter and sprinkle evenly on top of potato mixture. Bake at 350 degrees for 45 minutes. Ten servings.

ONE OF THE FEW FOODS I PREPARE IN THE MICROWAVE OVEN IS *acorn squash. The side dish is a good accompaniment to a ham dinner.*

Microwave Acorn Squash

2 acorn squash
4 teaspoons butter or margarine
4 tablespoons brown sugar
Cinnamon
$\frac{1}{3}$ cups walnuts, finely chopped

Poke each squash several times with a sharp knife. Be sure to poke deeply so the squash does not explode. Microwave on high about six minutes. Test the squash with the knife for tenderness. If it goes in easily, remove the squash from the microwave. If not, nuke another minute or two.

Cut each squash in half and scoop out the seeds. Fill each cavity with a teaspoon of butter, a tablespoon of brown sugar and a sprinkling of cinnamon and nuts. Return to microwave for about one minute, or until margarine and sugar melt. Serves four.

LANELL GRAHAM, DAUGHTER-IN-LAW MELISSA'S MOTHER, PREPARED *an immense casserole of her daughter's favorite dish, which was devoured by our family at a Thanksgiving celebration. The following year, when her mom and dad couldn't visit, Melissa took on the*

two-day task of preparing the dish and admirably upheld the family honor. Look for the dried green bell peppers in the spice section of the grocery.

Lanell and Melissa's Southern Stuffing

8 chicken breasts with bone in
6 small packages cornbread mix, such as Jiffy
Chicken broth, one cup or more
8 eggs, lightly beaten
1 pound butter, melted
½ to ¾ cup dried green bell peppers
⅓ cup dried onion flakes
1 package (12 ounces) herb-seasoned stuffing
    mix, such as Pepperidge Farm
2 teaspoons each salt and pepper, or to taste

Day 1: Boil chicken in water until tender, about 30 minutes. Cool. Pull off bones and shred. Save the broth. Refrigerate broth and chicken separately. Prepare cornbread according to package instructions.

Day 2: Crumble the baked cornbread. Heat one cup of reserved chicken broth. In a large bowl, mix the shredded chicken with eggs, melted butter, dried peppers, onion flakes, crumbled cornbread and stuffing mix. Pour enough hot broth over the mixture to make a thick cake batter consistency. You may need to add hot water if there is not enough broth. Add salt and pepper to taste.

Bake in two greased 9x13-inch pans at 375 degrees for 45 minutes or until golden brown. The stuffing will look like browned cornbread. About 18 servings. You can cut this recipe in half for smaller gatherings.

S ON GREG'S HIGH SCHOOL "COOKING" CONSISTED OF HEATING *frozen Steak-umms and Chicken Rondolets. You can imagine my surprise when he came home from college one Thanksgiving and offered to make a vegetable dish for the big meal. Without referring to a recipe, he transformed some carrots into a glossy masterpiece. Was I impressed!*

Americans, incidentally, eat a lot of carrots. In 2005, the average American ate 11.6 pounds of carrots – up from six pounds a year in the 1960s.

Greg's Orange-glazed Carrots

1 pound carrots (whole ones have better flavor,
    but you can save time using those packaged
    "baby" ones)
¼ cup orange juice
2 teaspoons cornstarch
2 tablespoons margarine
2 tablespoons light brown sugar
1 tablespoon orange zest
Freshly grated nutmeg (optional)

Scrape carrots and cut into strips (if using whole carrots). Bring large pan of water to boil and simmer carrots 10 to 15 minutes, until tender. If using "baby" carrots, cook a bit longer. Meanwhile, mix orange juice and cornstarch in a small bowl. In a large skillet melt margarine and add brown sugar, stirring until sugar dissolves. Add orange juice and cornstarch mixture and zest, and stir until thickened and glossy. Drain carrots and add to mixture, coating carrots well. Garnish with freshly grated nutmeg, if you wish. Four to six servings.

I DON'T KNOW WHERE GRANDMA GOT THE RECIPE FOR THIS RICH DISH. *We reserve it for holiday menus. Thrifty Grandma always bought a quantity of zucchini at the end of the summer, pared it, cut it and froze it for use at Thanksgiving.*

Grandma's Zucchini Casserole

3 pounds zucchini, peeled and cut in
    small chunks (about 6 cups)
1 large onion, chopped
2 sticks margarine
Salt and pepper
1½ cans (10½ ounces each) condensed cream
    of chicken soup
1 large carrot, grated
1½ cups sour cream
1 package (16 ounces) herb-seasoned stuffing,
    (crumbled type, not cubed), such as
    Pepperidge Farm

Cook zucchini and onion in a cup or two of water until tender. Drain. Place squash and onion in a large bowl and add one stick of margarine and salt and pepper to taste. Add soup, carrot and sour cream. Mix thoroughly. Melt second stick of margarine and mix into stuffing in another bowl. Add three-fourths of the margarine-stuffing mixture into the zucchini mixture and combine well by hand. Put into a 9x13-inch greased baking dish. Sprinkle remaining stuffing mixture over top. Bake 30 minutes at 325 degrees. About 12 servings.

H OMEGROWN TOMATOES AND ZUCCHINI TEAMED WITH VIDALIA *onions are an unbeatable combination. This is the ideal side dish for a cookout of steak, chicken or hamburgers. It is my standard*

potluck take-along. This recipe is an adaptation of one in my tattered copy of Keys to Our Kitchens, *the old Dayton Woman's Club book. The original recipe was submitted by an obviously good cook named Elise Biechler Gabriel. I would like to believe that her family appreciates the recipe as much as I do.*

Potluck Zucchini Casserole

6 medium zucchini, washed and sliced in
    $\frac{1}{4}$-inch thick rounds (do not pare)
6 large tomatoes, peeled and sliced
1 large sweet onion, such as Vidalia, sliced
    in thin rings
1 $\frac{1}{2}$ cups cracker crumbs, such as Ritz
1 cup sharp cheddar cheese, shredded
2 tablespoons dark brown sugar
Salt and pepper
$\frac{1}{2}$ cup butter, cut into small pieces

Grease a large casserole with margarine or cooking spray. Layer the dish with a portion of the zucchini, tomatoes and onions. Then sprinkle a portion of the brown sugar over the vegetable layers and follow with a sprinkling of salt and pepper, a portion of the cheese, a few pieces of butter and a portion of the cracker crumbs. Repeat the layers until the ingredients are gone, saving some crumbs for the top layer. Dot the top with remaining butter pieces. Bake at 350 degrees for 1 hour and 15 minutes. You can prepare this ahead of time, refrigerate and bake just before serving. Serves eight to 10.

G RANDPA SCHILLO AND MY FATHER WERE DEVOTEES OF OYSTERS, *which Grandma prepared only for Thanksgiving dinner. She continued making the dish long after Grandpa and Daddy were gone.*

Jenni and Greg nibbled on the cracker mixture, but shoved the oysters under a conveniently uneaten roll on their plate just as I did when I was a child. Now I consider this dish a delicacy. Serve it as an appetizer or a side dish. Garnish with sprigs of parsley.

Grandma's Scalloped Oysters

2 pints fresh oysters
2 cups saltines, crushed
1 stick butter, melted
¾ cup half-and-half
Parsley for garnish

Lightly grease a two-quart casserole. Rinse and drain the oysters. Place a layer of oysters in the casserole. Top with a layer of crushed saltines. Dribble with butter. Repeat layers, ending with cracker crumbs. Pour half-and-half evenly over all. Bake about 35 minutes at 350 degrees. Serves six to eight.

N EWLYWEDS HARRIET AND BILL MERRIMAN PARKED THEIR RENTED *U-Haul truck at the rear of the apartment and began lugging their furnishings up to the second floor. John Thomas and I were newlyweds, too, who had just moved into the North Canton, Ohio, complex, three weeks earlier. We greeted them at the top of the steps and offered to lend a hand. That day marked the beginning of a close friendship. In the mid-1960s, I was a novice cook, but Harriet had an innate culinary aptitude. She served this dish at a dinner party we co-hosted.*

Harriet's Party Peas

¼ pound margarine
½ cup onions, chopped
1 package (3 ounces) slivered almonds
1 cup fresh mushrooms, sliced

½ teaspoon garlic powder
1 tablespoon Worcestershire sauce
1 package (10 ounces) frozen peas
Salt and pepper to taste

In a skillet, melt the margarine and add onions and almonds. Cook about two minutes and then add mushrooms. Cook an additional two minutes. Add garlic powder, Worcestershire and frozen peas. Cook until peas are done, about four or five minutes. Add salt and pepper to taste. Four to six servings.

FOR THE PAST 10 YEARS, NANCY HINES AND I RITUALLY HAVE SHARED *new recipes during our bi-annual get-togethers. One year, I pulled out my favorite new recipe; it was corn pudding. Then Nancy went to her suitcase and plucked out her "recipe of the year." It was corn pudding, too. Here is her rich and delicious version.*

Nancy's Corn Pudding

1 can (16 ounces) cream corn
1 can (16 ounces) whole kernel corn
½ cup melted butter
8 ounces sour cream
2 large eggs, lightly beaten
1 package (8½ ounces) corn muffin mix, such
    as Jiffy

In a large mixing bowl, combine all ingredients. Pour into a greased two-quart baking dish. Bake at 350 degrees for 45 minutes, or until golden brown and a knife inserted in the middle comes out clean. (This can be baked in a 13x9x2-inch baking pan. The edges will be crispy, and it may take less than 45 minutes to bake.) Six servings.

GREG AND JENNI'S AUNT BETSY THOMAS WAS REARED WITH HER sister Carolyn and brother John in New Concord, Ohio, the burg that Astronaut John Glenn made famous. She later moved to Moscow, Idaho, which is known as the "Lentil Capital of the World." Betsy was highly respected in Idaho for her activities in support of women's rights.

I would guess that she became experienced at cooking the healthful lentils, but I remember her most for this broccoli and cheese casserole that she introduced to us in the 1960s.

Betsy's Broccoli Bake

2 packages (10 ounces each) frozen, chopped
   broccoli
¼ cup chopped onion
4 tablespoons melted butter or margarine
2 tablespoons flour
3 eggs, well beaten
8 ounces processed cheese in a jar, such as
   Cheese Whiz
½ cup cracker crumbs
Paprika

Cook broccoli according to package directions. Drain. Add onions, butter, flour, eggs and cheese. Stir well and turn into a medium-sized, greased casserole. Top with cracker crumbs and sprinkle lightly with paprika. Bake at 325 degrees about 30 minutes, or until slightly browned. About six servings.

THE FIRST THANKSGIVING AWAY FROM HOME CAN BE A HEART-tugging experience. When John and I married, we agreed to spend our first Thanksgiving with his family in his hometown of New Concord, Ohio.

His parents – Scott and Frances Thomas – and their relatives were country folk. Their table featured no frilly toothpicks with cheese or salamis like I had in my parents' home; there were no pink shrimp served in fancy goblets. But what they served was the most flavorful food in the world.

These families grew fields of food in the summer and expertly canned and froze their produce. The women in the family made the simple foods taste spectacular. With corn and lima beans from the freezer, Frances Thomas could make even succotash seductive. Her strawberry freezer jam shone like rubies on her fluffy biscuits. Her smooth gravy was perfectly seasoned.

But what I liked most of all was her cranberry sauce. In my parents' home, it came out of a can. Frances cooked fresh berries with tart apples, chilled the mixture and presented it in a cut-glass compote.

Frances' Cranberry Sauce

1 package (12 ounces) fresh cranberries
1 tart apple, diced
1 cup sugar
1 cup water

Mix berries, apples and sugar in a large saucepan. Add water and bring to a boil. Be careful! These berries pop. Cook on medium heat, stirring frequently, about 10 minutes or until the berries pop and the sauce thickens. If some berries are stubborn, mash them against the side of the pan until they pop. Cool and refrigerate several hours before serving. Six to eight servings.

ON SCHOOL DAYS, JOHN'S MOTHER COOKED LUNCHES FOR THE *students at New Concord High School, later renamed for John Glenn. But her best cooking was reserved for the family at home.*

One summer day, "Mom" walked into her kitchen with an apron full of green pods from the vegetable garden. She proceeded to wash them, slice them, bread them and fry them in hot grease. One bite and I was converted to a fan of okra.

Frances' Fried Okra

1 pound fresh okra
2 eggs, beaten
$\frac{1}{4}$ cup flour
$\frac{1}{2}$ cup cornmeal
$\frac{1}{2}$ teaspoon salt
$\frac{1}{4}$ teaspoon pepper
$\frac{1}{4}$-inch melted shortening in a skillet

Rinse okra, cut off stem ends and slice into $\frac{1}{2}$-inch rounds. Drop rounds into eggs and coat all sides thoroughly. In a separate bowl, mix together flour, cornmeal, salt and pepper. Drop egg-coated rounds into flour mixture and turn over so that each piece is covered with the mixture. Heat shortening and fry okra in skillet until golden brown. Serve immediately. Four to six servings.

Did you know that "fun" is the Chinese word for noodles? *Maybe that's why I like them so much. I dress up noodles with a variety of additions, but my favorite is poppy seeds.*

Noodles with Poppy Seeds

8 ounces broad noodles
2 tablespoons butter or margarine
1 tablespoon poppy seeds

Prepare noodles according to package instructions.

Drain. Melt butter in a skillet over medium heat. Add noodles and poppy seeds, stir and heat. Serves four.

WHEN SKIP AND JANIE BLOCK JOINED US IN ALASKA ABOARD *Kinship, it was apparent that Skip's cancer was advancing. He lacked the energy to explore ashore or to reel in salmon, but the retired Dayton surgeon professionally sprang to Jim's aid when he sliced his hand while cutting bait. We were thankful for his presence in this emergency.*

We also were pleased that Skip's appetite was intact and that mealtime remained one of his joys. One day, drawn by the aroma from the galley, he joined me as I was frying onions and cabbage. "Could you add some noodles to that, Joan?" he asked. "My mother always put noodles in the fried cabbage."

I complied, and this homespun dish was the focus of the meal. Surrogate son Jay Kyne, of Croatian descent, says his family called this dish "haluski."

Skip's Cabbage and Noodles

8 ounces noodles
2 tablespoons olive oil
$\frac{1}{2}$ head cabbage, shredded
1 medium onion, sliced fine
Salt and pepper to taste

Prepare noodles according to package directions. Drain and set aside. In a large skillet, heat the oil. Add cabbage and onions and sauté until the vegetables are soft, about 10 minutes. Add cooked noodles and salt and pepper to taste. Four servings.

The Meaning of Mishpocha

IN HIS BED UPSTAIRS WITH A CAPTAIN MARVEL COMIC IN ONE HAND and a crumpled tissue in the other, Jim sniffled and hacked. It wasn't fun being a sick kid, and it wasn't fair that he caught colds more often than anyone else in the family. He knew exactly what to expect on such days. His mother Florence would look him over and chide: "So! You're sick again! How many times have I told you to wear your jacket when it's cold outside."

Then she would go to the kitchen and mix the soothing milk and honey that comforted him. Sometimes, if the suffering son successfully elicited her sympathy, she would plop a chicken in a pot and prepare the Jewish mother's cure-all – chicken soup.

Of course, Florence Ungerleider wasn't a Jewish mother. She was an Irish Catholic – born a Graham. Although her first husband Dominic Darcy came from similar Irish background, her soul mate and second partner, Lou Ungerleider, had a Jewish heritage, and he hungered for the foods of his own family. Flossie adeptly adjusted her menus, and soon Lou proclaimed that his Catholic wife was the best Jewish cook in town. Her gefilte fish was tempting, and no one could make chopped chicken livers like Flossie.

Both Jim, a Catholic, and I, a Baptist, grew up in Dayton View neighborhoods that were heavily populated by Jews, and we were accustomed to eating Jewish fare – Challah bread, kugel and matzoh ball soup. On Grand Avenue where I lived, our neighbors included the Portneys, the Liebowitz's, the Liflanders.

ESTHER LIEBOWITZ, WHOSE KITCHEN WINDOW WAS JUST A FEW feet away from ours, would greet me in the mornings with an enthusiastic call, "Jo-Annnnn! Come over. I've got something for your breakfast." I'd pad to her back door in my slippers and babydolls, and she'd present me with half a cantaloupe filled with ripe berries from her husband's deli on Lexington Avenue.

My friends and I spent hours studying after school in one another's kitchens, and our mothers supplied the "noshes." Mother gave us sugar cookies and milk. Eileen Portney's mom provided matzoh and butter.

At Sandy Liflander's we'd carve a slice or two from the Kosher salami that dangled by a string on a nail near the back door.

Sandy and I were inseparable. I took turns spinning her dreidel at Chanukah and lingered at her house each evening during the holidays to watch her family light the menorah. At Passover, I could recite the miracle of the Red Sea parting and the history of unleavened bread almost as well as Sandy could.

YOUNG JIM GREW UP IN DAYTON VIEW

A S YOUNGSTERS, JIM AND I ABSORBED AN EXTENSIVE YIDDISH *vocabulary from our friends. When someone whispered about a neighbor's "zoftig" shape, we understood. When a friend's mother warned us to get off our "tokuses" and go outside to play, we got the message.*

Decades after our childhood, Jim and I realized that we spent our adult lives in neighborhoods devoid of ethnic diversity. But then, Penny Darcy emerged as a dynamic in our life. As Jim's brother's wife for some 20 years, Penny helped us revisit our past by cooking brisket and kugel and other Jewish specialties. "Oy vey," she "kvetched" as she "schlepped" the groceries in; but, in spite of her complaining, we knew that she took joy in the preparation of her old family recipes.

One night Jim and I sat around "schmoosing" about old times and people who played important roles in our lives. We couldn't think of an English word that suited the emotions we were feeling. And then we recalled the word "mishpocha." The Yiddish word remembered from our childhood conveys what we have been fortunate to experience throughout our lives — the comforting embrace of a magnificent mixture of family and friends.

WHEN PENNY DARCY COOKS BRISKET, SHE ALSO MAKES KUGEL. IN Yiddish, "lokshen kugel" means "noodle pudding." It tastes like dessert, but traditionally is served as a side dish.

Penny's Lokshen Kugel

1 ½ cups golden raisins
8 ounces broad noodles
⅓ pound salted butter
8 ounces creamed cottage cheese
8 ounces cream cheese
5 eggs
½ teaspoon cinnamon
½ teasoon nutmeg
¾ cup sugar
2 cups milk
1 teaspoon vanilla
Additional cinnamon

Soak raisins in hot water until soft. Drain them and set aside. Cook noodles al dente. Drain. Add butter. In a separate large bowl, mix cottage cheese and cream cheese and add the eggs and cinnamon, nutmeg, sugar, milk and vanilla. Stir cheese mixture and drained raisins into noodles. Place in a greased 9x13-inch baking pan and sprinkle top with cinnamon. Bake at 350 degrees 60 to 75 minutes, until a knife inserted in the center comes out clean. Let stand 15 minutes before cutting. Makes 12 servings.

IT TOOK ME 60 YEARS TO SAMPLE GNOCCHI. I GUESS I WAS WAITING *for the best place in the world to taste it – Rome. In a little trattoria near the Spanish Steps, Jim, Jack, Penny and I each ordered something different from the menu so we could experience several entrees. My gnocchi swimming in creamy Gorgonzola was voted best choice. In fact, we returned the next night so Jack could get a whole plateful for himself.*

When I returned to the United States, I developed my own version of the sauce. I buy ready-made, refrigerated gnocchi to speed up the preparation of the dish.

Quick Gnocchi with Gorgonzola Sauce

1 package (16 ounces) fresh, refrigerated
    gnocchi
1 tablespoon butter, melted
6 ounces Gorgonzola cheese, crumbled
1 cup half-and-half
Salt and pepper
$\frac{1}{4}$ cup Parmesan cheese, freshly grated

Cook the gnocchi according to package directions. While it is cooking, melt butter in a large skillet. Add crumbled cheese and the half-and-half, stirring until sauce thickens. Add salt and pepper to taste. Drain gnocchi and place in a serving bowl. Top with sauce and mix. Sprinkle Parmesan on each serving. About six servings.

I LOVE THE Food Channel ON CABLE TV, DON'T YOU? ONE DAY I HEARD *this easy tip for cooking cauliflower. I think that the recipe called for mushroom soup, but I like using cream of chicken.*

Easy Baked Cauliflower

1 head cauliflower, washed and trimmed,
    keeping head intact
1 can (10½ ounces) condensed cream of chicken
    soup

Place cauliflower in a greased baking pan. Dump the soup evenly over it. Bake at 350 degrees about 40 minutes, or until tender. Serves about six.

H ERE'S ANOTHER SUPER-EASY RECIPE. USE IT AS A SIDE DISH, OR *place it as a bed under grilled salmon or other fish.*

Sesame Spinach Saute

1 tablespoon olive oil
1 package (10 ounces) fresh spinach
1 tablespoon soy sauce
1 tablespoon sesame seeds

Heat the oil in a skillet. Add spinach and sauté until slightly limp – just a couple of minutes. Add soy sauce and sesame seeds and stir in thoroughly. Four servings.

Y OU CAN DRESS UP DEVILED EGGS WITH CAPERS, CRABMEAT OR BACON, *but I prefer Mother's old-fashioned combination of mayonnaise, mustard and celery seeds. I serve them on Grandma's well-used, cut glass plate that has indentations to hold the egg halves.*

Mother's Deviled Eggs

6 large eggs
⅓ cup mayonnaise
2 teaspoons prepared yellow mustard
½ teaspoon celery seed
⅛ teaspoon salt
Dash of pepper
Paprika

Place eggs in a saucepan in a single layer. Cover with water. Bring to a boil. Remove from heat and let stand 15 minutes. Drain and chill. Peel eggs and slice them in halves lengthwise. With a teaspoon, remove yolks and place in a small bowl. Mash yolks with a fork. Add mayonnaise, mustard, celery seeds, salt and pepper and blend well. Spoon the yolk mixture into the egg whites. Sprinkle paprika on each egg half. Six servings of two halves each.

J IM'S INVENTIVE FRIEND DAVE WYSE WOULD ACCEPT NO SUBSTITUTE *for dried minced garlic for his toasted garlic bread. Neither powdered garlic nor fresh would do. He liked the crunch of the dried garlic, and so do we.*

Dave's Garlic Bread

1 loaf Italian bread or other hearty bread

About 3 tablespoons butter
About 2 tablespoons dried minced garlic

Slice bread into pieces about ¾ inches thick. Spread butter on one side of each piece. Sprinkle garlic evenly on each. Place on a baking sheet in a preheated 400-degree oven for about 10 minutes, or until butter is melted and bread is lightly browned. About 10 servings, depending on size of loaf of bread.

THE FIRST TIME JIM AND I DINED AT CAMERON'S RESTAURANT IN *Worthington, Ohio, we joined Eric Kraut, a fellow oncologist at "The James." When we were served bread with a whole head of baked garlic and a small dish of jam, Eric demonstrated how to squeeze a garlic clove and spread it on the warm bread and top it with jam.*

Baked Garlic

6 whole heads of garlic
4 teaspoons olive oil
¼ cup water

Remove the papery outer skins of the garlic, but leave inner covering and the heads intact. Arrange the heads in a small baking dish and dribble the olive oil over the garlic. Put ¼ cup water in the baking dish. Cover with foil and bake in a 350-degree preheated oven about one hour until the garlic heads are soft. Serve one head to each guest along with hot bread and jam. Six servings.

MOTHER AND DADDY SELDOM BAKED BREAD. MOTHER REGULARLY *purchased white Wonder Bread, and Daddy, when he was flush, drove to the Schattschneider Bakery on Troy Street and came back with bags full of seedy pumpernickel, weighty Jewish rye and bumpy Challah. When Mother did bake bread, it was cornbread. It usually fell apart when we spread it with butter and apple butter.*

Mother's Iron Skillet Cornbread

1 cup yellow corn meal
1 cup flour
2 teaspoons baking powder
4 tablespoons sugar
¾ teaspoon salt
2 eggs
2 tablespoons shortening, such as Crisco, melted
1 cup milk
1 tablespoon butter

Sift and mix corn meal, flour, baking powder, sugar and salt. In a separate bowl, beat eggs with a whisk and mix with melted shortening and milk. Add this mixture to dry ingredients and beat well. Set aside.

Put butter into a 10-inch iron skillet or a 9-inch square baking pan and put in 425-degree preheated oven until butter bubbles. Pour cornbread mixture into hot pan and bake 20 minutes or until lightly browned. About eight servings.

OVER THE YEARS, I'VE MADE A LOT OF CORNBREAD. IT ALMOST *always fell apart like Mother's – until I stumbled onto this moist variation, sweetened with pudding mix.*

Sweet Cornbread

2 packages (9 ounces each) cornbread mix, such
    as Jiffy
1 package (4 ounces) instant vanilla pudding
    mix
2 large eggs
1 cup milk

In a large bowl, mix all ingredients by hand. Pour
into a greased 9-inch baking pan and bake about
25 minutes, until golden. Nine servings.

at 400°

Full Circle

FOUR-YEAR-OLD KYRA BOUNDED INTO THE KITCHEN. "LET'S BAKE *cookies, Grandma Joan!" Her words warmed my heart. Surely there is no honor greater than being identified as a cookie-baking grandma.*

Kyra, our first-born grandchild, has turned into a nutrition-conscious teenager. At one time, her favorite dish was pasta, but for years she would eat only Alfredo sauce. Now, she prefers a more healthful marinara. For a long time, her younger sister Tess readily named macaroni and cheese when asked to name her favorite meal, but she was hesitant when asked her favorite vegetable. After much consideration and eye-rolling, she would declare, "Well, I do eat carrots."

Cleveland cousin Cameron is broadening his food interests; he chooses Chinese when we go out to eat. At home, however, he prefers simpler fare: chicken fingers are an entrée of choice. Little sister Olivia will try most anything new. I remember when she was barely old enough to talk, she pointed to something green on her mother's plate and wanted to know what it was. Jenni offered her a bite and named the food. Little Olivia sampled it, and distinctly repeated the name with great appreciation: "Ah, guacamole," she said.

Cincinnati granddaughter Erika also has exhibited sophisticated tastes for a youngster. As a five-year-old, she snacked with pleasure on a plate of fresh raspberries and goat cheese. Her little brother Scott, however, seemed to subsist a year or two on yogurt and cottage cheese and salami, eschewing most greenery. Then out of the blue he would eat a big plate of green beans for dessert. Over time, as all the parenting books advise, he probably got the nutrition he needed.

Evan is among the youngest of our grandchildren. As a toddler, his eating habits baffle his parents. He chows down on tiny bits of the Paragon Restaurant's steak and shovels in the hash browns. But if the food is green, he rejects it. Much to his mother Kippy's chagrin, he also steadfastly refuses mashed potatoes.

The one grandchild who savors vegetables is Adriana, who became our eighth grandchild when Jason and her mother Rachel married. Teenage Adriana eats vegetables almost exclusively. Occasionally she will eat chicken as she did one evening when she offered Jim and me her specialty — made-from-scratch tamales. The menu required two days of cooking, involving boiling and shredding the chicken for the filling and mixing the masa into dough for the tortillas. She prepared sides of black beans and salad and served the meal like an experienced hostess.

Grandchild number nine, Madeline Joy, recently entered the world so it's way too soon to predict her food preferences. But we can expect that, like most children, she will go through stages that will frustrate her parents as they try to guide her to a healthful lifestyle.

J IM AND I REMEMBER THAT OUR OWN PARENTS TRIED DILIGENTLY *to introduce us to a range of foods. We heard the old admonitions: "Eat your spinach so you can be strong like Popeye." "Eat your carrots so you don't need glasses." And the familiar: "Clean your plate; think of all the starving children in China."*

We never, however, were told to eat fiber nor cautioned about the dangers of fat in our diet. Eating nutritiously meant having fried bacon and eggs every morning with toast or donuts on the side. Lunch was a hearty sandwich with meat and cheese, and dinner was planned around meat.

Generous supplies of butter and margarine were kept in my family's refrigerator. Margarine fascinated me. In the early 1940s, this white dairy product came packaged in plastic with a red capsule sealed inside. You squeezed the bag until the capsule broke, and then you worked the mass until it was transformed into a yellow butter look-alike.

Our refrigerator shelves held Braunschweiger (also known as liverwurst), yellow boxes of Velveeta and squat jars of Limburger cheese, which was consumed by only men in our family. They spread it on crackers and topped it with sliced onions, a highly aromatic snack that repulsed any self-respecting woman.

Hungry visitors had to be alert when they looked for a snack in my parents' refrigerator. They might mistake a jar of Mother's ironing starch for vanilla pudding. Or worse, they might expectantly lift the lid of a Chinese carryout carton and find fat earthworms that Daddy kept on hand for impulsive fishing trips.

WHEN I WAS A GIRL, SHOPPING FOR FOOD WAS A FORM OF *family entertainment. Mother and I made weekly rounds in the Dayton Arcade – our city's predecessor to the modern mall. The corridor leading to our food emporium was lined with small shops.*

On our way to food shopping, Mother and I peered into the plate glass show window of the millinery store where we bought our Easter bonnets. The spring styles came in pastel shades with touches of tulle and daisies and roses. The fall styles featured luxurious fabrics with bird feathers and imitation gems. Once Mother bought a pillbox to wear to a dinner party. It was fashioned of black velvet with a dark veil sprinkled with satin dots. She was movie-star glamorous in that hat.

We often stopped at the shoe repair shop to have Daddy's soles replaced or to have half-moon metal taps nailed to my saddle shoes so the heels would last through the school year.

Then we crossed the canopied alley and entered the food market. The Arcade had highly specialized concessions – one booth for soft pretzels, one for fresh peanut butter, another for vegetables. The friendly hubbub of the place reverberated under an imposing paneled glass dome above our heads.

THE MOST COMPELLING SIGHTS WERE THE MEAT AND FISH *counters, which extended the width of the building. There were stacks of sleek catfish with broad heads and feelers intact, piles of pie-faced halibut and flounder, and mountains of monstrous carp.*

Bib-aproned butchers with boxy white caps perched on their heads hoisted slabs of ribs and weighty roasts for close inspection. With giant ladles, they dipped out slippery oysters from deep vats. Here you could get dressed ducks and live turtles for your family feasts.

I was a child mesmerized by the honey-comb-patterned tripe. Despite the appealing appearance, Mother disdained this meat. But she bought other organ foods – liver and kidney, and brains too. She bought scallops for special meals that Daddy would prepare, round steak for goulash, drumsticks for my meal and wings for her own.

On our trips downtown, Mother also bought candy. She craved candy. We bought it at the Gallaher drugstore near the Arcade. Bulk candies occupied center stage in this store. We walked round and round the glass display cases to deliberate about our selections. From the chocolate area, we chose chocolate-covered raisins and hand-dipped caramels. In the chewy section, I selected orange slices and gummy spearmint leaves. Mother liked puffy orange "circus peanuts." We bought wrapped candies, too — saltwater taffy from Atlantic City and root beer barrels. Both of us adored "mothballs" — filberts coated with a sugary crust. We emerged from the store with six or seven tiny white paper bags, each containing a fourth-pound of our favorites, and as soon as we boarded the Lexington Avenue bus for home, we sampled a piece from every bag.

Now I bask in my nostalgia and wonder if it is a profligate use of time. No, I decide, it is not. I'm convinced that these recollections will help me prepare for the visits of the grandchildren. Yes -- we will have such fun. We will shop for gummy bears and M&Ms, roll out cookies and make wonderful memories as I fulfill my honorable role as Grandma.

Children's Choices

THE FIRST "RECIPE" I REMEMBER PREPARING AS A CHILD WAS *stuffed dates, and to this day, I love them. Both walnuts and dates are nutritious, of course, but I suppose that licking my fingers after rolling them in sugar is what hooked me.*

Walnut-Stuffed Dates

18 large pitted dates
18 walnut halves
Confectioner's sugar

Open the dates and insert walnut piece. Close and roll in confectioner's sugar. Makes 18 pieces.

GIVING FOOD A CUTESY NAME IS A PARENTAL TRICK PASSED DOWN *over generations. Kids might snub these snacks if you call them "stuffed celery," but name them "Bugs on a Boat" and you might get a taker.*

Bugs on a Boat

Celery ribs, cleaned and cut into 3-inch pieces
Cream cheese or pimiento cheese
Raisins or dried cherries

Spread cheese in wells of celery and line the top of the cheese with raisin or cherry 'bugs."

IN THE DAYS WHEN MY CHILDREN WEREN'T EAGER TO EAT SALADS, THEY *looked forward to taco-building nights. I lined up the ingredients*

in various bowls, and they piled on the lettuce and tomatoes. This is son-in-law Andy's recipe for the one dish he claims to have mastered. With supervision, even young children can help prepare this meal and choose the toppings they like best. You might even be able to slip in some chopped green or red peppers. Guacamole is a good addition too.

Andy's Taco Delight

1 ½ pounds ground beef
1 package taco seasoning
Lettuce, chopped
Tomatoes, chopped
Onions, chopped
Cheddar cheese, shredded
8 flour tortillas

Brown beef in a skillet and drain the grease. Place meat in a strainer and rinse the meat with water. Return to the skillet and add seasoning packet and prepare according to directions of the package. Meanwhile, place tortillas on aluminum foil on a cookie sheet. Place wet paper towel on top and warm in low (250 degrees) oven about 10 minutes. Place on serving dish and layer lettuce with ground meat, tomatoes, onions and cheese. Fold over. Eight servings.

EVEN PICKY CHILDREN EAT PIZZA SO THEY MIGHT ENJOY THIS NON-*traditional pizza, which is smothered with raw vegetables. It also is popular as an appetizer at adult gatherings. Nancy Greer brought the snack to a potluck lunch at the former Schonberg Associates' office in Dayton.*

During the holidays, I form the dough into the shape of a Christmas tree and let grandchildren help "decorate" the tree with vegetables.

Bits of broccoli look like evergreen, carrot rounds and green onions make good ornaments, and thin strips of red bell peppers serve as garlands. Top the tree with a cheese star.

Nancy's Veggie Pizza

1 tube (8 ounces) refrigerated crescent rolls
1 package (8 ounces) cream cheese, softened
$\frac{2}{3}$ cup mayonnaise
1 teaspoon dried dill weed
$\frac{1}{2}$ teaspoon garlic salt (optional)
Fresh vegetables cut into small pieces (onions, carrots, broccoli, cherry tomatoes, mushrooms)
$\frac{1}{3}$ cup shredded cheddar cheese

Press crescent rolls into a pizza pan or shape as you wish on a baking sheet. Bake eight minutes in a preheated 350-degree oven. The crust is ready when it is lightly browned. Cool the crust. Mix mayonnaise and cream cheese in a small bowl. Spread on the cool crust. Sprinkle with dill and garlic salt. Arrange vegetables on top and sprinkle with cheese. About eight servings.

JENNI AND GREG GREW UP IN THE "PEPSI GENERATION" ERA, BUT *it might as well have been dubbed the "pizza generation." They consumed pizza for dinner and lunch, and they ate leftover pizza for breakfast. It's easy to understand why this recipe, with its Parmesan and oregano flavors, was popular with their teenage friends.*

Greg and Jenni's Teen Party Snacks

1 8-ounce tube refrigerated crescent rolls
2 tablespoons margarine, melted

$\frac{1}{4}$ cup grated Parmesan cheese
1 or 2 teaspoons crushed, dried oregano
Dash garlic powder
8 hot dogs
Wooden toothpicks

Separate dough into four rectangles and press perforations closed. Brush each with melted margarine. In a small bowl, mix cheese, oregano and garlic powder and sprinkle over the dough.
Cut each rectangle of dough crosswise to form a total of eight squares. Place hot dog on each square and roll up, stretching dough as needed to cover. Cut each roll into three pieces, securing each with a wooden toothpick. Bake 12 to 15 minutes on an ungreased cookie sheet in a preheated 375-degree oven. Serve hot. Makes 24 snacks.

THE CHILDREN WILL HAVE FUN DISCOVERING THE "SPAGHETTI" *inside the squash. After you cook it, let them pull out the strands. Spaghetti squash is also delicious with butter and freshly grated nutmeg stirred in.*

Magic Spaghetti

1 spaghetti squash
1 $\frac{1}{2}$ cups prepared marinara sauce, such as
    Prego
Parmesan cheese, grated

Poke several holes in the squash with a sharp knife. (Caution: be sure to cut deep slashes or squash will explode. Believe me, I know about this!) Microwave it on high five minutes. Then cut the squash in half crosswise; place each half on a plate, cut side down, and microwave another five minutes. Remove seeds with a spoon. Using a fork, pull some of the strands. If they do not release easily, microwave another few minutes until tender strands can be easily pulled away from the skin. Then remove all spaghetti-like strands and place in a serving bowl. Top with marinara sauce and grated cheese. Serves four to six, depending on size of the squash.

THESE CUPCAKES ARE IDEAL FOR TODDLERS' BIRTHDAY PARTIES. *Young children can handle them easier than conventional cupcakes in paper wraps.*

Ice Cream Cone Cupcakes

1 package cake mix of your choice
24 cake cones with flat bottoms
2 cans prepared frosting of your choice
Sprinkles

Prepare cake batter according to package directions. Set cake cones upright in muffin tins. Fill each one-half to two-thirds full of batter. Bake according to directions for cupcakes on the package. Frost and garnish with sprinkles. Makes 24 cupcakes.

HELEN HOKE AND I AND OUR FOUR CHILDREN OFTEN ATE LUNCH *together when we lived side by side on Lynnfield Drive in Kettering, Ohio. The kids eagerly ate Helen's pastry-enclosed hot dogs. This batter is also exceptionally good for deep-frying onion rings and other vegetables, particularly zucchini and fresh button mushrooms.*

Helen's Pronto Pups

8 hot dogs
1 cup flour
1 ½ teaspoons baking powder
2 tablespoons cornmeal
½ teaspoon salt
3 tablespoons shortening, such as Crisco
1 egg, beaten
¾ cup milk
Vegetable oil

Put flour, baking powder, cornmeal and salt in a bowl. Cut in shortening. Stir in egg and milk until the mixture is smooth. Dip hot dogs in batter, allowing excess batter to drip off into bowl. Pour vegetable oil in a large saucepan to a depth of about three inches. Heat the oil until a tiny bit of batter dropped in sputters and browns quickly. Then fry the hotdogs two at a time until golden brown. Serves eight.

FARMERS' SODAS" WERE HIGHLY ANTICIPATED SUMMER REFRESHMENTS *at Grandma's house. If we didn't have ice cream, we simply mixed equal amounts of ice cold milk and cream soda. I haven't any idea how they got their name.*

Farmers' Sodas

2 scoops vanilla ice cream
Red cream soda

Put ice cream into a tall glass and pour cream soda over the top. Eat the froth with a spoon; then add more soda and a straw. Serves one.

WHEN YOU VISITED AUNT THELMA'S HOUSE OVER THE HOLIDAYS, *you went back home with a goody bag filled with homemade popcorn balls. Here's how she made them for years.*

Aunt Thelma's Marshmallow Popcorn Balls

6 tablespoons butter or margarine
3 cups tiny marshmallows
1 package (3 ounces) raspberry gelatin
3 quarts unsalted popped popcorn

In a medium saucepan, melt butter or margarine over medium low heat. Add marshmallows; stir until melted. Blend in dry gelatin. Pour over popped popcorn and mix well. With buttered hands, form into 12 balls. Wrap in wax paper or plastic wrap. Makes 12 treats.

MOTHER TAUGHT ME THE INTRICACIES OF CANDY MAKING. I LEARNED *about soft-ball and hard-ball stages and other information you need to know to keep candy from falling apart or endangering your teeth. But one candy was so easy and foolproof that any child could make it. She called it Chinese candy because chow mein noodles supplied the crunch.*

Mother's Chinese Candy

1 can (14 ounces) chow mein noodles
½ cup peanuts, chopped
¾ cup butterscotch chips
¾ cup semi-sweet chocolate chips

Place noodles and nuts in a medium bowl. In a double boiler or in the microwave, melt the butterscotch chips and the chocolate chips together, stirring until smooth. Quickly mix them into the chow mein noodles and nuts. With a tablespoon, drop the mixture into patties on a sheet of wax paper. Cool until set. Makes about 20 pieces of candy.

WHEN THEY WERE YOUNG TEENS, SISTERS CHRISTY, KATIE AND *Amy Baxter from Columbus, Ohio, taught us that you don't need a campfire to make s'mores. (Be sure to sing a round of Kumbaya when you eat these.)*

Microwave S'mores

Graham crackers split into squares
Mini marshmallows
Plain chocolate bars, such as Hershey's

Place several mini marshmallows on a graham cracker square. Top with a piece of chocolate bar. Place a graham cracker on top. Lay on a sheet of wax paper. Put into microwave and heat on high about 30 seconds, until chocolate and marshmallows melt and mingle.

CHILDREN WILL LOVE DIPPING THESE CANDIES AND EATING THEM *too. You can teach them a little history while you are making them: In 1953, Ohio adopted the buckeye as the state tree. Its name, the story goes, dates back to the Native Americans comparing the likeness of the "nut" to the eye of a deer, thus "buckeye." This recipe appeared many years ago in Mildred Urban's cooking column in the* Kettering-Oakwood Times. *She reported it was from the recipe file of co-worker and friend, Mickey Pieper.*

Mickey and Mildred's Buckeyes

1 stick butter at room temperature
1 pound confectioner's sugar
1 cup peanut butter
1 teaspoon vanilla

Mix the ingredients and place in the refrigerator two hours. Then form the mixture into small balls, the size and shape of buckeyes. Return to the refrigerator for two more hours.

Chocolate Coating
1 package (12 ounces) semi-sweet chocolate chips
$\frac{1}{2}$ cake paraffin

Melt chocolate chips and paraffin in a double boiler; stir until smooth. With a toothpick, pick up each peanut butter ball and dip it three-fourths of the way into the chocolate, leaving an uncovered light spot to resemble a buckeye. Place on wax paper to cool and harden. Makes about two dozen candies.

Note: You find paraffin in the grocery aisle where canning supplies are displayed. You can melt the ingredients in the microwave in a bowl, but do watch the mixture closely.

THE FIRST CHRISTMAS ADRIANA WAS PART OF OUR FAMILY, THE *then 11-year-old surprised us with a festively wrapped package of cookies that she made herself. These shortbread cookies are divine. We have added them to our list of traditional holiday fare.*

Adriana's Shortbread

4 cups flour
1 cup sugar (do not substitute no-calorie
    sweetener)
1 pound cold butter (do not use margarine)

Combine flour and sugar in a large bowl. With a
pastry blender or two forks, cut in the butter until
the mixture is crumbly and fine. Knead the dough
until smooth. This will take a while – six to eight
minutes.

Press the dough into an ungreased 15x10-inch
baking pan.

With a fork, pierce the dough all over. Bake in a
preheated 325-degree oven for 25 minutes, until
light brown in color. While warm, use a sharp knife
to cut into 48 squares.

Index